100 Greatest Ideas . . . in an instant!

Whether you're a first time manager or an experienced leader, running a small team or an entire organization, straightforward, practical advice is hard to find.

John Adair's 100 Greatest Ideas . . . are the building blocks for an amazing career, putting essential business skills and must-have thinking at your fingertips.

The ideas are short, punchy and clustered around themes, so you'll find answers to all your questions quickly and easily. Everything you need to be simply brilliant is here, and it's yours in an instant.

Look out for these at-a-glance features:

Personal Mantra –
Powerful statements as a source for inspiration

Ask Yourself –
Questions to get you thinking about the most information

Remind Yourself –
Key points to help you reflect on the Ideas

Checklist –

A list of questions to help you put the Ideas into practice

100 Greatest Ideas . . . 6 Great Books

John Adair's 100 Greatest Ideas for Effective Leadership

John Adair's 100 Greatest Ideas for Personal Success

John Adair's 100 Greatest Ideas for Brilliant Communication

John Adair's 100 Greatest Ideas for Smart Decision Making

John Adair's 100 Greatest Ideas for Amazing Creativity

John Adair's 100 Greatest Ideas for Being a Brilliant Manager

JOHN ADAIR'S

100

GREATEST

IDEAS

FOR *SMART*

DECISION MAKING

CAPSTONE

This edition first published 2011
© 2011 John Adair

Registered office
Capstone Publishing Ltd. (A Wiley Company), The Atrium, Southern Gate, Chichester, West Sussex, PO19 8SQ, United Kingdom

For details of our global editorial offices, for customer services and for information about how to apply for permission to reuse the copyright material in this book please see our website at www.wiley.com.

Library of Congress Cataloguing-in-Publication Data

9780857081759 (paperback), ISBN 9780857082220 (epub), ISBN 9780857082237 (emobi), ISBN 9780857082169 (ebook)

A catalogue record for this book is available from the British Library.

Set in 10 on 13 pt Calibri by Toppan Best-set Premedia Limited

Printed in Great Britain by TJ International Ltd, Padstow, Cornwall

Author's Note

Effective business people have fine-tuned leadership and management ability backed up by exceptional decision-making, communication and creative skills and the know-how to implement it all successfully. These six areas are the basis of the 100 Greatest series.

None of these skills stands alone, each is interconnected, and for that reason I've revisited key ideas across the series. If you read more than one book, as I hope you will, you'll meet key ideas more than once. These are the framework on which the series hang and the repetition will help you become a master of modern business.

Likewise, if you only read one book, the inclusion of key ideas from across the series means that you'll benefit from seeing your chosen subject within the wider context of Leadership and Management excellence.

Good luck on your journey to becoming an effective manager within your organization.

John Adair

Contents

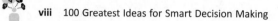

Preface

Success in any field depends on your ability to make the right decisions all the time. None of us get it right all the time, but this book will help you to learn valuable lessons from your own mistakes and – what is much less costly – the mistakes of others.

The basic unit of the book is the Idea. These Ideas are clustered together under themes and divided into five Parts.

As you will see, an Idea varies considerably from covering just one simple big thought to being a 'cluster bomb' of smaller ideas for improving the related activities of decision making, problem solving and creative thinking.

The Ideas are all independent of each other, like prose poems. So this isn't the kind of book that you have to start at the beginning and read through until you come to the end. Find an Idea that looks interesting and then work your way out from there.

Think of the Ideas as a hundred oysters, collected in a basket for you from the floor of the world's ocean. Now it is all up to you. To coin a proverb, *God gives you the oysters, but you have to find the pearls.* Good luck!

John Adair

PART ONE

Effective Thinking Skills

The development of general ability for independent thinking and judgement should always be placed foremost, not the acquisition of special knowledge.

Albert Einstein, German physicist

Behind your practical, everyday thinking there lies the most complex thing in the known universe: the human mind. Nobody hires and pays you nowadays for your physical strength. You are employed because you have a mind – and can use it effectively.

There are three forms of applied thinking that we all need: decision making, problem solving and creative thinking. These overlap considerably but they can be distinguished from one another:

1. Decision making is about deciding what action to take, which usually involves choosing between different options.
2. The objective of problem solving is usually to find a solution, answer or conclusion.
3. The outcome of creative thinking, by contrast, is new ideas.

Any leader who aspires to excellence obviously has a vested interest in seeing that the best decisions are taken, that problems are solved in the optimum way and that the creative ideas and innovations so necessary for tomorrow's business flow freely.

As Roy Thompson, a great business entrepreneur, once said, 'If I have any advice to pass on, as a successful man, it is this: if one wants to be successful, one must think; one must think until it hurts.' He added, 'From my close observation, I can say that there are few people indeed who are prepared to perform this arduous and tiring work.' Are you one of them?

Thirteen Greatest Ideas on How Your Mind Works

Idea 1: Inside your head

Every head is a world.

Cuban proverb

The physical base of your mind is of course your brain, the grey matter housed in your head. Your brain is composed of about 10,000 million cells. In fact, it has more cells than there are people on the face of the earth! Each one of those cells can link up with approximately 10,000 of its neighbours, which gives you some 1 plus 800 noughts of possible combinations.

Amazing, isn't it? But there is more:

◆ At any one moment your brain is receiving about 100 million pieces of information through the ears, eyes, nose, tongue and touch receptors in the skin.

◆ It consumes about 10 watts of power per day. If scientists tried to build a brain of silicon chips, they think it would need around 1 million times more power than the human brain.

◆ If you were to stretch out all the nerve connections in our brain, they would reach a distance of about 3.2 million kilometres.

Before we go any further, I would like to double check that your brain is fully switched on. See if you can solve both parts of the following problem within 30 minutes – the world record is 9 minutes.

Who owns the zebra?

1 There are five houses, each with a front door of a different colour, and inhabited by people of different nationalities, with different pets and drinks. Each person eats a different kind of food.

2 The Australian lives in the house with the red door.

3 The Italian owns the dog.

4 Coffee is drunk in the house with the green door.

5 The Ukrainian drinks tea.

6 The house with the green door is immediately to the right (your right) of the house with the ivory door.

7 The mushroom-eater owns snails.

8 Apples are eaten in the house with the yellow door.

9 Milk is drunk in the middle house.

10 The Norwegian lives in the first house on the left.

11 The person who eats onions lives in the house next to the person with the fox.

12 Apples are eaten in the house next to the house where the horse is kept.

13 The cake-eater drinks orange juice.

14 The Japanese eats bananas.

15 The Norwegian lives next to the house with the blue door.

Now, who drinks water and who owns the zebra?

Time's up. How have you got on? Now turn to the Appendix, where I talk you through the best way of solving this problem.

'The more difficult a problem becomes, the more interesting it is.'

Idea 2: The mind at work

A picture is worth a thousand words.

Chinese proverb

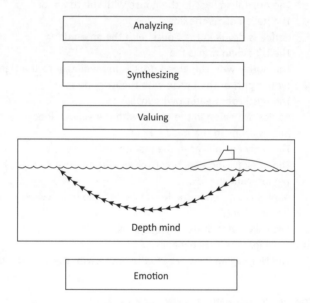

When you are thinking to some purpose there are three principal mental functions at work:

Analyzing – resolving wholes into their constituent parts
Synthesizing – building wholes out of their different elements
Valuing – judging or appraising on scales of relative worth

These activities take place on various levels of the mind. Sometimes they submerge like a submarine into the *depth mind* (the unconscious) and resurface later on.

We think as whole persons, not as disembodied minds. Therefore *emotion* or *feeling* is ever present, waiting in the wings. It plays a positive or negative role in the drama of thought.

Idea 3: Your depth mind

There is a great deal of unmapped country within us.

English proverb

The phrase 'the unconscious mind' is very familiar. Following popular expositions of the theory of Sigmund Freud, who did more than anyone else in modern times to put the unconscious mind on the map, we tend to think of the unconscious as a kind of dustbin for our early personal frustrations. Into it drops all our mental rubbish: the bruised egos, the damaged wishes, the broken loves, the resentments, fears, hatreds and rages of our childhood.

We then force down the lid on these suppressed feelings. But they erupt again in our dreams and in various forms of behaviour, such as the celebrated 'Freudian slips'. We have to remember, however, that Freud based his conclusions on his study of mentally ill patients.

To counter this rather negative image of the unconscious, later Freudian psychologists felt it necessary to coin yet another word: the *preconscious*. This stands for the realm where helpful subliminal thinking takes place, and is roughly equivalent to my own term, the *depth mind*.

The metaphor of *depth* here is drawn from the analogy of the sea. The *conscious* mind is like the surface; the *subconscious* is the depth of a few fathoms where the light penetrates; while the *unconscious* is the deeper recesses into which we cannot see.

Case study: C. S. Forester

As a novelist C.S. Forester is perhaps best known for his sequence of stories about Horatio Hornblower, a British naval officer in the era of the Napoleonic wars. In this extract from an autobiographical account of his early years, the author reflects on creation and the part played in creation by the unconscious or depth mind:

> In my own case it happens that, generally speaking, the initial stimulus is recognized for what it is. The casual phrase dropped by a friend in conversation, the paragraph in a book, the incident observed by the roadside, has some special quality, and is accorded a special welcome. But, having been welcomed, it is forgotten or at least ignored. It sinks into the horrid depths of my subconscious like a waterlogged timber into the slime at the bottom of a harbour, where it lies alongside others which have preceded it.
>
> Then, periodically – but by no means systematically – it is hauled up for examination along with its fellows, and, sooner or later, some timber is found with barnacles growing on it. Some morning when I am shaving, some evening when I am wondering whether my dinner calls for white wine or red, the original immature idea reappears in my mind, and it has grown.
>
> *Long Before Forty* (Michael Joseph, 1967)

Far from being a marginal and outdated quality, intuition is central to the way successful thinkers work.

Therefore encourage intuition in yourself. Become more aware of it. Be more receptive to its often faint whisper. Always subject it to evaluation, however. Granted that safeguard, intuition can save you a great deal of time in decision making.

Idea 4: What the depth mind can do

While the fisher sleeps the net takes the fish.

Ancient Greek proverb

The functions of the conscious mind – analyzing, synthesizing and valuing – can also take place on a deeper level. Your depth mind can dissect for you, just as your stomach juices can break down food into its elements.

The depth mind, for example, is capable of analyzing data that you may not have known you had taken in, and comparing it with what is filed away in your memory bank.

The depth mind is capable of more than analysis. It is also close to the seat of your memory and the repository of your values. It is also a workshop where creative synthesis can be made by an invisible hand.

An organic analogy for its function is the womb, where after conception a baby is formed and grows from living matter.

You may also have experienced the value of thinking of the depth mind's neighbour that we call conscience in the form of feelings of guilt or even remorse. Conscience is useful, because its red light may tell you that your decision making has led to a wrong move.

Intuition is the power or faculty of immediately apprehending that something is the case. It seems to occur without any conscious reasoning. And there is plenty of evidence that effective decision makers do listen to their intuition.

At its best, intuition works because more information is going into your mind through your senses than your faculties at their conscious level can process. So your depth mind does some informal analyzing, synthesizing and valuing, and an intuition that occurs in the conscious mind is one of its products.

If an intuition comes to you after a longish period of time it is likely to be more reliable; if it comes very early in the story, take your time in checking it out.

> *There is a dark*
> *Inscrutable workmanship that reconciles*
> *Discordant elements, makes them cling together*
> *In one society.*
>
> William Wordsworth

Idea 5: Become aware of your depth mind

Unconscious thought, there is the only method: macerate your subject, let it boil slow, then take the lid off and look in – and there your stuff is, good or bad.

Robert Louis Stevenson, author of *Treasure Island*

The first step to making productive use of your depth mind is becoming more aware of its powers.

One of the daily wonders of the mind, for example, is how we can recall things so swiftly on demand. If you are asked a fact, such as someone's name, you may often say (if you are like me), 'Give me a minute or two and I'll remember it.' A few minutes later the name pops into your conscious mind. Amazing.

Memory as our private data bank plays a central part in our thinking, but is not the only contribution of the depth mind to effective mental activity. The most interesting manifestation of the depth mind is to be found in all forms of human creativity.

No one knows quite how the depth mind goes about its work. We do know, however, that it is capable of carrying out all the principal functions of the mind – analyzing, synthesizing and valuing – on a subliminal level, and then 'announcing its findings' to the conscious mind.

The depth mind can both supply you with the seed of an idea and carry out an often intricate process of synthesis for you over a period of time. Both contributions are present in this passage by Lewis Carroll:

I was walking on a hillside, alone, one bright summer day, when suddenly there came into my head one line of verse – one solitary line – 'For the Snark was a Boojum, you see'. I knew not what it meant, then: I know not what it means, now: but I wrote it down: and, some time afterwards, the rest of the stanza occurred to me, that being its last line: and so by degrees, at moments during the next year or two, the rest of the poem pieced itself together . . .

Can we develop this immense reserve power of our depth mind? Yes, within reason. Some people are more gifted in that way than others. But awareness of the part played by the subconscious, coupled with a friendly interest in how it works, can set you on the path to self-development.

Using your depth mind in sleep

You may have had the experience of 'sleeping on' some decision or problem and finding that your mind has made itself up the next morning. If you haven't, give it a try. The depth mind principle can also be used to memorize material. Just before you go to sleep, read what you have to learn, preferably out loud, and as you settle down, concentrate on the material. As soon as you wake up, try to recall what you read – you may be surprised at how much you have remembered.

Idea 6: Checklist – Listening to your depth mind

- ☐ Do you have a friendly and positive attitude to your depth mind?
- ☐ Do you *expect* it to work for you?
- ☐ Where possible, do you build into your plans time to 'sleep on it', so as to give your depth mind an opportunity to contribute?
- ☐ Do you deliberately seek to employ your depth mind to help you:
    - ☐ Analyze a complex situation?
    - ☐ Restructure a problem?
    - ☐ Reach value judgements?
- ☐ Have you experienced waking up next morning to find that your unconscious mind has resolved a problem or made a decision for you?
- ☐ Do you see your depth mind as being like a computer?
- ☐ Remember the computer proverb: *Garbage in, garbage out.*
- ☐ Do you keep a notebook or pocket tape-recorder at hand to capture fleeting or half-formed ideas?
- ☐ Do you think you can benefit from understanding how other people's depth minds work?

Idea 7: Learning to trust your intuition

*There is no logical way to the discovery of these elemental laws.
There is only the way of intuition, which is helped by a feeling
for the order lying behind the appearance.*

Albert Einstein, German physicist

Intuition is the most common general word for the faculty of the
depth mind. It indicates the kind of comprehension or knowledge
that comes quickly into your mind, apparently without the intervention of conscious reasoning, inferring or deliberation.

The most characteristic example of intuition is when you come to
know – or suspect – that a situation exists when you have no direct
evidence that it is the case.

Managers are often deterred from recognizing and using their own
intuitive powers because they feel that, somehow, intuition is not
intellectually respectable. They certainly believe that it is not scientific enough. The cult of the rational manager has an iron grip on such
minds. But this idea is nonsense. Some of the most celebrated scientists have been intuitive in their work.

If you are now inclined to be more aware of intuition when thinking
and to give it more status, you have already taken the first step
towards making better use of it. The next step is to learn to trust your
intuitive powers. That does not mean always, nor does it mean occasionally, because one cannot generalize about how often.

Nevertheless, you should be prepared to give your intuition the
benefit of the doubt; you should build up a warm and friendly relationship with that part of your mind that is prepared to offer you this
unique service.

Idea 8: How intuitive are you?

Intuition is awareness that a situation exists when reason or logic – if consulted – might say that it was improbable or even impossible. Do you have such awareness:

Rarely	☐	Sometimes	☐
Frequently	☐	Never	☐

- ◆ In your judgement of people, do you tend to rely on first impressions? Are they usually right?
- ◆ Do you often 'feel' your way to a decision or a solution to a problem?
- ◆ Do you sometimes find it difficult to explain your intuitions to others?
- ◆ When your intuitions turn out to be wrong, in hindsight why is this so?

Case study: Paul Getty

When I first started drilling in the Oklahoma oil fields the consensus of expert judgement held that there could be no oil in the so-called Red Beds region. But like so many oilmen, I chose to temper all 'analytical' thinking with a healthy dose of non-logical subjectivity. To me, the area looked as if it might hide oil. Largely on the basis of a hunch, I decided to see for myself. I began drilling in the Red Beds, struck oil and brought in a vast new producing field. I rather suspect that by relying upon such non-textbook thought processes and taking attendant risks, the biggest fortunes have been made – in oil and other endeavours.

Business flair is a consistent theme in the lives of great industrialists and merchants. They intuitively spot an opportunity for making money. They can smell a potential profit where others can see nothing but present losses. It is an instinct that is separate from the dictates of reason or logic that guide more plodding minds. When it is not followed, such business people often realize their mistake later.

Alfred Sloan, perhaps the greatest manager of his day, once worked with William C. Durant, the founder of General Motors. He recalled that Durant 'would proceed on a course of action guided solely, as far as I could tell, by some intuitive flash of brilliance. He never felt obliged to make an engineering hunt for facts'. Sloan concluded: 'The final act of business judgement is intuitive.'

Idea 9: Intuition at work

Read the following brief account and consider the questions that follow.

Case study: Golda Meir

Mrs Golda Meir, former Israeli Prime Minister, once said that she caused the initial debacle in the 1973 Yom Kippur War, and ruined her political career, because she ignored her own intuition.

In her autobiography, the Russian-born and American-raised woman who became Israel's Prime Minister noted that when, on Friday, 5 October 1973, news was received that the Russian advisers were leaving Syria in a hurry, 'I tried not to become obsessive. Besides, intuition is a very tricky thing. Sometimes it must be acted upon at once, but sometimes it is merely a symptom of anxiety.'

She was reassured by Moshe Dayan, then Minister of Defence, Chief of Staff and Chief of Intelligence. They did not think war was imminent. Nor did General Bar Lev, former Chief of Staff.

She added: 'Today I know what I should have done. I should have overcome my hesitations that Friday morning. I should have listened to the warnings of my own heart and ordered a call-up. For me, that fact cannot and never will be erased and there can be no consolation in anything that anyone else has to say.'

Ask yourself

Do you agree that Mrs Meir should have acted on her intuition that Friday morning?

Can you identify an episode in your own life when you had an intuition on which you failed to act? What were the consequences?

Idea 10: Conscience

A clear conscience never fears midnight knocking.

Chinese proverb

Our capacity to have values is universal. A person who lacks the faculty to value would not be a person.

We differ, of course, in the values themselves – the products or constructs of our valuing minds. Our values are reflections of our ideas of what is morally good or right: they supply us with the moral principles for our conduct in life.

The depth mind is the seat of conscience, the rather specialized faculty that tells you – often retrospectively – that you have done something very wrong.

Far from it being a bad conscience, as it is sometimes called, it is a good conscience doing its proper work.

Whether or not you choose to respond to what your depth mind dictates is a secondary issue. The result of not heeding your conscience is that its loud call becomes a whisper, and one day you will not hear it at all.

I suggest that the depth mind can analyze and value as well as synthesize. In the former respect it can be compared to your stomach, which contains powerful enzymes that can break down the meals it is fed. The analogy of digestion, the process of making food absorbable by dissolving it and breaking it down into simpler chemical compounds, seems especially apt.

With regard to valuing, it is again impossible to be precise about what goes on. What is clear, however, is that our values inhabit our deeper minds and are often obscure to us until we do something or have to choose between two alternatives.

Rationally we may believe (quite rightly) that decisions should be made on the basis of our values. Nevertheless, it is often the case that the decision comes first, and that tells us something about what our values really are.

That is why you should judge an organization's values not by any written or oral declaration of them, but by what the organization actually does. *By their fruits you shall know them.*

There is another related phenomenon here, namely that sometimes and for some people the very act of decision in itself seems somehow to confer value – 'Because I have chosen Smith as branch manager he must be good' or, at a more serious level, 'Because we decided to invade Iraq it must have been the right thing to do.'

Valuing is a human faculty – we all have it. What we call our values constitute one of the results of exercising this faculty. They differ widely, of course, because we as societies and individuals vary so much too.

Idea 11: The whole person thinks

Thought is not a trick, or an exercise, or a set of dodges.
Thought is a man in his wholeness wholly attending.

D.H. Lawrence, author of *Sons and Lovers*

Thinking is often contrasted with emotion or feeling. In reality the mind is one, it contains both elements. It is not surprising, therefore, that there is a complex relationship between thinking and emotion.

Emotion, along with motive, concerns things that move us. Emotion is the partly mental, partly physical response of being stirred up by someone or something. Physical danger or threat produces a stirring of emotion: strong feelings of fear and physiological changes that prepare your body for immediate, vigorous action. If prolonged, such experiences may add up to stress.

The word *emotion* carries a stronger implication of excitement or agitation than *feeling*, which suggests that our most powerful emotions lie dormant in the depths of our minds and are only stirred up on rare occasions. Emotions are rather like strong winds, raging thunderstorms or blazing heat, while feelings are breezes, showers or the warmth of sun on skin.

Negative emotions or feelings, such as hatred or fear, anxiety or worry, can play havoc with our thinking processes. That is why calmness is so important in a decision maker.

Yet positive feelings can enhance our intellectual powers. Love in particular is a great teacher in how to think. And without the feeling of interest, the mind would be like a computer without electricity.

Sometimes dolphins lead mariners to safety. Sometimes, too, thinkers report the sensation of pleasure *before* they make a significant discovery – feelings that are the dolphins of the mind.

Less poetically, psychologists call this phenomenon the *hedonic response*.

Remind yourself

To be an effective thinker and decision maker you need to be able to control your emotions and feelings, not be controlled by them.

'Nothing in life is to be feared, it is only to be understood.'

Idea 12: Valuing

Truth is the language that identifies what is universal.

Antoine de St Exupéry, French novelist

According to an ancient Roman proverb, *Integrity is the noblest possession*. Integrity implies trustworthiness and incorruptibility to a degree that one is incapable of being false. A person of integrity prizes truth above all else.

Establishing the truth – the realities of the situation – is always a necessary condition for effective decision making. Not that it is easy. Indeed, in some situations truth may be hard to come by.

When making decisions we often need to consult specialists who have the necessary professional or technical knowledge. Nevertheless, it is not wise to accept what they say without question. Here is another use of your valuing skills: you need to evaluate the advice you are given by a specialist.

You can see now that your ability as a decision maker depends largely on your judgement, and judgement in turn is mainly a function of your values and your valuing skills.

For a good leader, truth is not just factual accuracy – reflecting reality – although that remains important. It also involves trustworthiness, reliability and straightforwardness.

Idea 13: Know your mind

Eureka (Greek *heureka*) means 'I have found it'. Today we use it as an exclamation of delight at having made a discovery. Archimedes, the Greek mathematician and inventor, originally uttered it when he discovered how to test the purity of Hiero's crown.

The story is that Hiero, the king of Syracuse, gave some gold to a smith to be made into a crown. On receiving it back, he felt its weight and his suspicions were aroused. Had the smith fraudulently alloyed it with an inferior metal? But he couldn't prove anything. So he asked Archimedes to devise a test for its purity.

The philosopher did not know how to proceed. He gave the matter a great deal of thought, but still a solution eluded him. Then one morning he got into his bath, which was full to the brim. He noticed at once that some of the water spilled over. Immediately the principle came to him that as a body is immersed it must displace its own bulk of water.

Silver is lighter than gold, he reasoned. Therefore a pound weight of silver is bulkier than a pound weight of gold and would consequently displace more water. Thus he found a simple method to establish if the crown was deficient in gold. As an early writer records:

When the idea flashed upon his mind, the philosopher jumped out of the bath exclaiming 'Heureka! Heureka!' and, without waiting to dress himself, ran home to try the experiment.

Ask yourself
Can you identify in this story four identifiable phases of creative thinking: preparation, incubation, insight and validation? (There's more on this in Idea 80.)

Have you ever had a similar experience? (I don't mean rushing naked through the streets!)

Eight Greatest Ideas for Clear Thinking

Idea 14: Analytical ability

The product of a good analytical mind should be clear thinking. That is why strategic leaders throughout the world placed *analytical ability* in seventh position on this list of 25 attributes:

Ranking of most valuable attributes at the top level of management

1 Ability to take decisions	13 Enterprise
2 Leadership	14 Capacity to speak lucidly
3 Integrity	15 Astuteness
4 Enthusiasm	16 Ability to administer efficiently
5 Imagination	17 Open-mindedness
6 Willingness to work hard	18 Ability to 'stick to it'
7 Analytical ability	19 Willingness to work long hours
8 Understanding of others	20 Ambition
9 Ability to spot opportunities	21 Single-mindedness
10 Ability to meet unpleasant situations	22 Capacity for lucid writing
11 Ability to adapt quickly to change	23 Curiosity
12 Willingness to take risks	24 Skill with numbers
	25 Capacity for abstract thought

> *'Wise leaders do not do anything unless they are clear in their mind first.'*

Idea 15: Hallmarks of a good analytical mind

How do you spot a good analytical mind in a team member or in someone applying for a job? First, we have to define what we mean by analytical ability.

Many people think of analysis more or less in its original literal meaning of simply taking things to bits, like a child dismantling a toy. But in the conceptual realm of the mind it is much more than that – when analyzing you are looking for something, rather like dissecting a dead fish to inspect its backbone. What your intellectual quarry actually is will depend on the nature of the case, but you may, for example, be seeking to:

◆ Establish the *relationship* of the parts to each other and to the whole.
◆ Find the true *cause* or causes of the problem.
◆ Identify the *issue* at stake, the 'either–or' on which a decision must rest (what a good trial judge does).
◆ Discover a *law* in nature.
◆ Search for the *principles* behind experience.

These general points can be illustrated by examples drawn from particular fields:

Chemistry	The resolution of a chemical compound into its elements and any foreign substance it may contain.
Optics	The resolution of light into its prismatic constituents.
Literature	The critical examination of any production, so as to exhibit its elements in simple form.
Grammar	The determination of the elements composing a sentence or part of it.
Mathematics	The resolving of problems by reducing them to equations.
Philosophy	The breaking down of complex expressions into simpler or more basic ones.

Ask yourself
Can you call to mind one individual you have worked with who impressed you with their analytical ability? Can you identify what distinguished them?

Idea 16: How to achieve clarity

Desire happiness from a good day's work, from illuminating the fog that surrounds us.

Henri Matisse, French artist

The path to becoming a clear thinker is not an easy one. The best method is to try to eliminate any *lack* of clarity. Start with your own thoughts and speech: it is always wiser to remove the bush in your own eye before you tackle the leaf in your neighbour's.

You won't be short of work, because the enemies of clarity are legion. They include thinking that is sloppy, inconclusive, blurred, cloudy, muddy, confused, doubtful, foggy, fuzzy, muddled, obscure, unclear, unintelligible or vague.

One tip to remember is not to confuse clarity with precision. As Aristotle said in his *Ethics*: 'It is a mark of the educated person that in every subject he looks for only so much precision as its nature allows.' Every increase in clarity has intellectual value in and of itself. An increase in precision or exactness has only a pragmatic value as a means to some definite end in a particular problem.

Idea 17: The power to simplify

When the solution is simple, God is answering.

Albert Einstein, German physicist

Analytical ability stresses the power to simplify: either what is complex or complicated (as by separating it into its constituent parts), or what is chaotic and confused (as by a reorganization that shows the relation of the details to each other and the whole).

In derogatory use *analytical* may imply a tendency to multiply sub-divisions unnecessarily, but in favourable or more neutral use it points to the power to systematize, clarify and interpret. It is distinguished from the power to create or invent.

The essence of all science is trying to reduce things to a few simple rules so that the human mind can understand it.

Simplicity is an elusive, almost complex thing. It comes from discipline and organization of thought, intellectual courage – and many other attributes more hard won than by short words and short sentences. For plain talk – honest plain talk – is the reward of simplicity, not the means to it. The distinction may seem slight, but it is tremendously important.

Unattributed

'Everything should be made as simple as possible, but not more simple.'

Idea 18: Asking the right questions

I keep six honest serving-men
They taught me all I knew;
Their names are What and Why and When
And How and Where and Who.

Rudyard Kipling, author of *The Jungle Book*
and the *Just So Stories*

Kipling's famous 'serving-men' are not only good teachers, they can also be great tools for achieving clarity.

Think of them as a sculptor's chisels. You can use them to chip away at a block of information until the shape inside it – the inner reality – becomes clear and visible. It is only by asking the right question, and only sometimes by repeating it three times, that you get at the truth.

Case study: Churchill and R.V. Jones

During his period as Prime Minister during the Second World War, Sir Winston's favourite 'boffin' – a scientist employed by the government – was a young, softly spoken scientist called Dr R.V. Jones. The Prime Minister would summon him from the headquarters of MI6 across St James's Park.

Reg Jones made his great breakthrough on 21 June 1940. With his team he had been puzzling over radio beams transmitted from Germany during bomber raids over England and became convinced they were a navigation device for steering aircraft to their targets. Some senior scientists were highly sceptical, refusing to believe that beams could be bent around the earth's surface. Jones believed they could and, what is more, that they could be bent again by countermeasures in order to redirect the aerial raiders away from urban areas to drop their bombs over open country.

Jones made a lasting impression on the Prime Minister. Thereafter Churchill swore by him as 'the man who broke the bloody beam'; heady stuff for a 28 year old.

'The first thing was to be absolutely scrupulous in trying to establish the truth,' Jones said as he recollected his meetings with Churchill. 'Winston said: "You don't have to be polite, you just have to be right." If you got somebody, however eminent, and asked him three successive "Whys?", there were not many people who could stand up to it. It was quite astonishing how shaky their knowledge base was. It was the old story of 99 per cent perspiration and one per cent inspiration. One needed a very sound grounding in basic principles and a mistrust of elaborate argument when something simple would do.'

The standard set by both Churchill and Jones – to be absolutely scrupulous in trying to establish the truth – is a high one and calls for teamwork in any organization. But nothing less than attaining that standard should be your first aim if you seek excellence in business leadership.

'No problem can withstand the assault of sustained questioning.'

Idea 19: The untrapped mind

The 'untrapped mind' is open enough to see many possibilities, humble enough to learn from anyone and everything, perceptive enough to see things as they really are, and wise enough to judge their true value.

Konosuke Matsushita, Japanese industrialist

A trap is a contrivance of some kind for catching animals so that they are prevented from moving. An untrapped mind is one that is free to move. It is 'in the clear'. Matsushita identifies four of its qualities:

Openness	Being responsive to a wide range of possibilities, new ideas, suggestions, and opportunities.
Humility	Being ready to learn from anyone, regardless of their status, and everything – failures and disappointments as well as successes.
Perception	Being able to see with a clear eye things, people and ideas as they really are.
Wisdom	Integrating one's judgement of value with one's clear thinking and creative orientation.

Ask yourself
If you had to add a fifth quality to this list, what would it be?

Idea 20: The skill of clear thinking

He who thinks too much about every step he takes will stay on one leg all his life.

Chinese proverb

To improve your decision-making capability you need to become a clear thinker. Can you call to mind three people you have met who have a reputation for clear thinking?

The way to improve your skills as a clear thinker is to challenge all that appears to be – in your own thinking or that of others – sloppy, inconclusive, blurred, confused, doubtful, foggy, fuzzy, muddled, obscure, unclear, unintelligible or vague. You won't be short of work!

There is a link between having a good analytical mind and being a clear thinker. You have to be able to reduce a complex problem or situation to its essentials.

What you need is the ability to think for yourself, as if from first principles. That requires a balance of confidence and humility: confidence in your own intellectual powers and humility that keeps you from that fatal form of overconfidence known as arrogance.

Questions play a key part in clear thinking. Indeed, sometimes finding the right question to ask is more important than anything else at the time.

Beware of 'paralysis by analysis'. If a decision needs to be made, you should always identify *when* it has to be made. Overanalyzing situations is as bad as not giving them sufficient thought in the first place.

Idea 21: Think for yourself

One day the mother of England's famous poet Shelley was discussing her son's future education.

'Why not send him somewhere where they will teach him to think for himself?' her friend suggested.

'Teach him to think for himself? Oh, Heavens above, teach him rather to think like other people,' she replied, in horror at the thought.

None of us can entirely escape thinking like other people, for society couldn't exist without some common patterns of thoughts and values. But the phrase *thinking for oneself* suggests someone with an independent mind or attitude.

To be independent of mind means that you don't depend on any other person for your essential opinions. You never bestow on any authority the right to control your mind – your thoughts, beliefs and attitudes – without any questioning on your part.

If you think for yourself you may be wrong, of course, but at least they will be *your* mistakes and errors, not those of other people. And the benefit of this approach is that you will take full responsibility for them and not pass the blame on to others.

Ask yourself
Do I try to think things out for myself, working from first principles?

Five Greatest
Ideas for Truth

Idea 22: The love of truth

The faintest of all human passions is the love of truth.

A.E. Houseman, English poet

The University of Oxford once saw fit to bestow on me a higher degree. In the company of a gowned throng I attended the Sheldonian Theatre to receive it. During the long ceremony my eyes wandered up to the allegorical painting on the ceiling. Done by King Charles II's court painter Robert Streater, it depicts Truth descending on the Arts and Sciences to expel ignorance from the university.

It is a noble vision and one that has inspired countless great minds in arts and sciences down the centuries. Take, for example, Yaq'qub ibn Ishaq al-Kindi, one of the great polymaths of Islam's medieval 'golden age'. He could declare:

> We should not be ashamed to recognize truth and assimilate it, from whatever quarter it may reach us, even though it comes from earlier generations and foreign peoples.
>   For the seeker after truth, there is nothing of more value than truth itself; it never cheapens or debases the seeker, but ennobles and elevates him.

Coming down to a more practical level, the necessary condition for all successful decision making and problem solving is being able to perceive the truth – *being able to see things as they really are*. Seeing reality, knowing what corresponds to reality, is always the thinker's first aim. It should be the rock-like foundation for action.

A *fact* is something that has really occurred or is known to be true or existing, as distinct from an inference. Notice the connection between fact and truth, between reality and truth. It helps to make truth less mystical, to bring it down to earth.

'Get the facts and then act.'

Idea 23: A rock for decision makers

He who is a slave of truth is a free man.

Arab proverb

Establishing the truth – or the reality – of a situation is the essential preliminary to knowing what is the best thing – or the least worst thing – to do.

Decisions based on wishful thinking, false assumptions, undetected errors, careless calculations, faulty figures or vain assurances are hardly likely to succeed, except by the unreliable intervention of luck.

A true leader will always speak the truth, for then their people will see the reality of the situation. Helping groups and organizations to do so and to respond appropriately lies at the very heart of leadership, especially in testing times. Consider the following story.

Case study: La Valette

Jean Parisot de la Vallete, the 72-year-old Grand Master of the Knights of St John who commanded Malta during the great siege by an immense force of Turks three centuries ago, was such a leader. On hearing the news that there was no hope of an early relief, he read this dispatch to his Council:

We now know that we must not look to others for our deliverance! It is only upon God and our own swords that we may rely. Yet this is no cause for us to be disheartened. Rather the opposite, for it is better to know the truth of one's situation than to be deceived by superficially sound but empty hopes.

La Vallete is surely right, but it is not always easy to follow his good example. The situation can be extremely complex. That is why you need to develop your ability to think clearly.

'It is better to know the truth of your situation than to be deceived by false hopes.'

Idea 24: Integrity

Integrity is the noblest possession.

Roman proverb

Field Marshal Lord Slim defined integrity by its effects: 'It is the quality which makes people trust you.' But what is it about integrity that induces that feeling?

The word itself means entireness, wholeness, soundness. It is a holistic word. You might be tempted to conclude that integrity as such does not exist; perhaps it is the pattern of all your moral qualities. For it implies a unity that indicates an independence of parts and the completeness and perfection of the whole.

Nevertheless, there are some distinctive elements. Integrity implies adherence to a code of moral, artistic or other values. It suggests, too, trustworthiness and incorruptibility to a degree that one is incapable of being false to a trust, responsibility or pledge.

At the core of integrity lies the value of truth. It is hard to overemphasize the value of truth in any form of thinking.

Its most common synonym is *honesty*, the refusal to lie, steal or deceive in any way. These qualities of character rest on the assumption that you can perceive the truth in a situation. If you build your decisions on truth, you are like a man building his house on rock. That is why you need integrity to be a good decision maker.

For decision making rests on two pillars:

1. Establishing the truth.
2. Knowing what to do.

Because managers are prey to time pressures and tend to be action oriented anyway, they are inclined to skimp on the first pillar and move too quickly on to the more congenial second.

If you act on the assumption that there is a truth 'out there' you will struggle until you find it, knowing that only decisions based on truth are likely to be successful. We certainly know that the converse is true: if a decision is based on faulty evidence it is unlikely to be successful.

Ask yourself
- ◆ Can you identify a situation at work where you would be compelled to resign on grounds of conscience?
- ◆ Have you ever, in your career, refused to tell a lie and borne the consequences?
- ◆ Do you act as if you believe that truth is 'out there' when you are thinking?
- ◆ 'Truth is great and shall prevail, when none care whether it prevail or not.' Do you think that the truth has a power or life of its own, that it will assert itself if only you allow it to do so?

You can see now that your ability as a decision maker depends largely on your judgement, and judgement in turn is mainly a function of your values and your valuing skills.

For a good leader truth is not merely factual accuracy, reflecting reality, although that remains important. It also means trustworthiness, reliability and straightforwardness.

I never encourage deceit; and falsehood, especially if you have a bad memory, is the worst enemy a fellow can have.

The fact is truth is your truest friend, no matter what the circumstances are.

US President Abraham Lincoln, in a letter
to George E. Pickett, 22 February 1841

Idea 25: The principle of falsification

Madam, a thousand experiments cannot ever prove me right;
a single experiment can prove me wrong.

Albert Einstein, German physicist

The epigraph is Einstein's reply to a woman who was rather effusively congratulating him on news of an astronomical observation that seemed to prove his theory of relativity.

The philosopher Karl Popper formulated his famous principle of falsification mainly from his conversations with Einstein. The fact that a scientific generalization could be falsified, Popper argued, was precisely what made it a proper scientific hypothesis.

Science advances by making conjectures (hypotheses and later theories), which are tested by empirical experiment and perhaps refuted; if refuted, they are replaced by further conjectures until eventually conjectures are found that are not refuted by tests.

Universal claims, such as scientific ones, can be much more easily falsified than verified. For example, to falsify the claim that 'all comets travel in elliptical orbits', you only need to find a single comet that doesn't travel in an elliptical orbit.

Theories that survive all tests that attempt to disprove them over time gather grounds under them for holding them (a purist would add, provisionally) to be true. For example, we now hold the theory of evolution to be true.

Einstein extended the principle of falsification beyond science by suggesting that social theories – to use shorthand – are falsified by experience in much the same way that scientific theories are tested by empirical experimentation. Those that survive the tests of time merit being considered as true. As the English proverb says, *Truth is the daughter of time.*

Remind yourself

It is easier to prove that something is not true than to establish that it is true. So at least you can now avoid making that mistake!

Idea 26: 'As if' thinking

Truth is like the sun. You can shut it out for a time, but it ain't going to go away.

US singer Elvis Presley

Does truth – or Truth – exist? I really don't know. Nor does anyone else. What we *know* and what we *believe* are two different things.

What is a fact, however, is that when people act *as if* truth existed and that it was there to be discovered – we never *make* truth, we find it – the results have been spectacular. I am thinking mainly of science, although the principle applies in other fields.

In other words, the conviction that truth exists 'out there' seems to work for us. It is a heuristic tool. From the Greek verb meaning 'to find', heuristic applies to something that is in itself unproven or incapable of proof but yet is a valuable means or instrument for finding things out.

The practical belief that truth in the form of the universal laws of nature is 'out there' to be discovered has paid off in science. You can adopt it, too. It makes you alert to look for something and not to be satisfied until you have found it. You may be sceptical but you are not cynical. You have the right attitude.

> *'Truth is the language that identifies what is universal.'*

Follow-up test

Effective thinking skills

☐ Can you think of anyone who has achieved a degree of personal success who lacks good judgement in their business?

☐ Would you describe yourself as good at visualizing things you haven't directly experienced yourself?

☐ Has anyone praised you for your imagination within the last year?

☐ Have you invented or made anything recently, at work or in your leisure time, that definitely required imagination?

☐ Do you tend to foresee accurately what happens before the event?

☐ Where possible, do you build into your plans time to 'sleep on it', so as to give your depth mind an opportunity to contribute?

☐ Do you deliberately seek to employ your depth mind to help you to:

◆ Analyze a complex situation?
◆ Restructure a problem?
◆ Reach value judgements?

Clear thinking

- ☐ Has anyone commented in the last year on your clarity of mind?
- ☐ Apart from your analytical skills, are you also able to think holistically, to see the whole wood and not just the trees?
- ☐ Have you experienced waking up the next morning to find that your unconscious mind has resolved a problem or made a decision for you?
- ☐ Do you see your depth mind as being like a personal computer? Remember the computer proverb: *Garbage in, garbage out.*
- ☐ Do you think you can benefit from understanding how other people's depth minds work?
- ☐ Can you think of three instances when you have trusted your intuition and acted on it?

Truth

- ☐ In an argument about what to do, does the love of truth guide you, or is winning more important?
- ☐ Do you always prefer to know the reality of your situation, or to be deceived by specious hopes?
- ☐ How important for you is the quality of intellectual integrity when you are choosing people to be managers?

PART TWO

Decision-Making Strategies

Men sleep well in the Inn of Decision.

Arab proverb

When chief executives throughout the world were asked to rate 25 attributes in order of importance, they put *Ability to take decisions* first, followed by *Leadership, Integrity* and *Enthusiasm*, in that order (see Idea 14).

Part Two focuses on the well-established logical or step-by-step process of making a decision. There are five constituent chords that you need to be able to master, though you may not always play them in the logical sequence that common sense suggests.

Previous generations, with their emphasis on rational models, tended to ignore the purposive activity of the depth mind. We now know that it plays a much larger role in decision making than they assumed. Your depth mind, for example, has often decided before your conscious mind is even aware of the fact!

It is simple to consider an individual making a decision in the first instance, but at work we are characteristically sharing decisions with others. As a leader you need to understand the options open to you, and develop the kind of judgement that enables you to choose the right one in the given circumstances.

Twenty-two Greatest Ideas for Decision Making

Idea 27: Decisiveness

There is a time when we must firmly choose the course we will follow, or the relentless drift of events will make the decision.

US President Franklin D. Roosevelt

Decisiveness is an important leadership quality. You do need to be able to take the responsibility for making a decision – the right decisions at the right time and in the right way.

Don't confuse being undecided with being indecisive. Being undecided is the state you are in before you take a decision; being indecisive is chronic dithering after the time when you know you should have taken a decision.

Case study: US President Woodrow Wilson

I made up my mind long ago, when I got my first executive job, to open my mind for a while, hear everybody who came to me with advice, information – what you will – then, some day, the day when the mind felt like deciding, to shut it up and act. My decision might be right; it might be wrong. No matter, I would take a chance and do – something.

Notice that phrase, *the day when the mind felt like deciding*. In other words, Woodrow Wilson had learned to listen to his depth mind, confident that it would tell him when the time had come to decide – and perhaps, too, when it was ready with a decision for him to take.

'A leader must not only be decisive,' wrote Ordway Tead in *The Art of Leadership* (1935), 'he must impress his followers with the fact that a decision has been reached and that hesitation, vacillation and questioning are over. He must *act* in a decided way and support his decision with a confident and courageous attitude. He must *look* decided.'

> 'You must not only be decisive, you must look decisive.'

Idea 28: Five steps in making a decision

1. *Define the objective* – Having recognized the need for a decision, specify the aim or objective.
2. *Identify the factors* – The factors are any circumstance, fact or influence that contributes to a result.
3. *Develop options* – List possible courses of action; generate ideas.
4. *Evaluate and decide* – List the pros and cons; examine the consequences; measure against relevant criteria; undertake trials; test against objectives; select the best.
5. *Implement* – Act to carry out the decision; monitor the decision; review the decision.

Idea 29: Thinking clearly about objectives

Our plans miscarry because they have no aim. When man does not know what harbour he is making for, no wind is the right wind.

Seneca, Roman philosopher

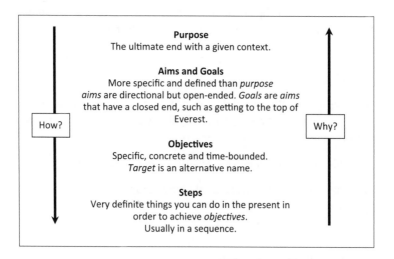

Deciding on objectives is like that fabulous ladder in Jacob's dream in Genesis (28:12), stretching from heaven to earth, with angels descending and ascending.

Descending

Descending Jacob's ladder, from the general and abstract to the particular and concrete, you are answering the question 'How?' This is my *purpose*. Yes, but *how* are you going to achieve it? By tackling these *aims* or *goals*.

Notice that *aims*, as defined above, are really no more than *purpose* broken down into manageable parts. It is like light being refracted into the colours of the rainbow.

The same is true of the next stage in the descent. Take any one *aim*. How are you going to achieve it? Answer: by achieving these *objectives*.

Now pick out any of these *objectives*: how are you going to accomplish that? Answer: by taking these *steps*. Today? Yes, there's bound to be one of those *steps* that you can take right now!

Upwards

Going upwards rather than downwards, you are then answering the question 'Why?' Why are you taking this *step*? In order to achieve this *objective*.

Why this *objective*? To move along that *aim* or towards that *goal*.

Why that *aim/goal*? In order to fulfil my *purpose*.

 Remind yourself
The most obvious advantage of thinking in this way is greater flexibility. If you think in terms of *purpose* you can more easily alter your plans as circumstances arise. Remember that Columbus was sailing for India when he discovered America. Because his purpose was to *explore*, we do not regard him as a failure.

Idea 30: What is information?

A critical factor in any decision is ultimately the information on which it is based. What is information?

Information usually applies to a kind of knowledge gathered from various sources (by observation, from other people or books, for example) and accepted as truth. The term carries no specific implication regarding the extent, character or soundness of that knowledge. Often, indeed, it suggests no more than a collection of data or facts, either discrete or integrated into a body of knowledge.

Facts, by contrast, are pieces of *information* that are known by observation or proof to be true or real.

Data (actually the plural of datum, a Latin form, but now often used in the singular) is a formal word for a large body of facts or figures that have been gathered systematically and from which conclusions may be drawn. The amassing of *data* is usually for scientific and statistical purposes, and the *information* obtained is often fed into a computer for rapid processing.

Ask yourself
◆ Given the nature of *information* as set out above, how would you go about discerning the facts of the situation as opposed to false assumptions?
◆ How would you distinguish the *relevant* facts, data and information from all the *irrelevant* material?

Idea 31: The time/information curve

Suppose that the overlap between information *required* and information *available* is not sufficient: what do you do? Obviously you set about obtaining more of the information in the *required* category. But getting information or – to us a grander description – doing research incurs costs in time and money. Your organization may not be in the business of making profits, but it certainly has to be businesslike when it comes to containing costs.

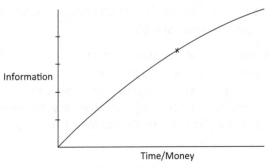

Time/Money

The time/information curve

What the graph suggests is that you can usually acquire a great deal of relevant information in a relatively short time and, possibly, at a relatively low cost in money.

For example, if you and I sat next to each other at a dinner, I should be able to learn all the really important things about you in the first half hour – all the information *required*. The longer we talked, the smaller the increments of knowledge about you would become. After three hours I should be down to discussing relatively fine details, and we'd be in the realms of information *available*.

Idea 32: Factor analysis

To see what is in front of your nose requires a constant struggle.

George Orwell, author of *Nineteen Eighty-Four*
and *Animal Farm*

A factor is a circumstance, fact or influence that actively contributes to a result. When making any significant decision, there will be factors that have a direct or indirect bearing on that decision. Here are some practical suggestions:

◆ List and name (or identify) all the major factors that are self-evidently important, and those minor ones that could have some influence on the achievement of the aim. For example, a general may have to consider the parties' relative strengths, ground, time and space, climatic conditions, security and courses open to the enemy.

◆ Continually ask yourself when weighing up a factor: 'So what?' If the answer does not add up to much, then the factor is not worth considering. The answer to the question 'So what?' is a deduction. Vague and indecisive deductions are not of much use: deductions must be clear, definite and relevant. In other words, each factor must be 'squeezed dry' until it has yielded all it has to give.

◆ Search for the critical factor, the one on which the making of the decision really hinges. It is not always there, but seeking it is a valuable way of turning over the ground.

◆ Look at all the factors taken together. Here synthetic thinking comes into play to balance undue concentration on one factor or set of factors. The combined influence of all the factors, the mysterious sum of the situation that is more than all its parts, needs to be sensed or felt.

Again, both value thinking and the depth mind can be heavily involved in the consideration of factors. Obviously our own values and the values of other individuals, the organization or society can be factors in their own right, and may well turn out to be the critical factor.

Provided that we do not disturb its work with worry or anxiety, the depth mind is adept at the holistic work of seeing factors as a whole.

Ask yourself
◆ Have I identified all the relevant factors that influence this decision?
◆ Is there a key factor on which everything turns?

Idea 33: Develop options

Decision implies real choice. The more feasible the options you have to choose from are, within the broad constraints of time and space, the better your decision is likely to be.

Even if there appears to be one course open once the truth has been established, an experienced manager will cast around in their mind to see whether there is another option.

Case study: There is no alternative

It was 17 September 1862. Cannon thundered along the battle lines as two armies of blue and grey soldiers faced each other across the Antietam Creek. Then General Ambrose Burnside gave the order to advance. The Union army was to storm across the creek and attack the enemy at close quarters. The route he chose to send them led over the narrow bridge across the creek, the only one in the vicinity. The Confederate gunners in the batteries specially placed to command the bridge could hardly believe their eyes. They swept away regiment after regiment with grapeshot. The slaughter was appalling.

General Burnside had failed to discover that the Antietam Creek in this region was only about 3 feet deep. It could have been forded by infantry or cavalry at any point with perfect safety. Of the battle at Antietam and the general who lost it for him, President Lincoln said somewhat bitterly: 'Only he could have wrung so spectacular a defeat from the jaws of victory.'

Burnside had acted on the assumption that he had only one option open to him. In fact we now know that he was wrong. He had not carried out a thorough reconnaissance. His decision rested on an erroneous understanding of his situation.

Considering options is inseparable from gathering information about the situation. As you scan a situation, analyzing and sifting it, you will see the more obvious possibilities for action. In the second phase of thinking, when you have grasped the essentials of the problem or situation, you switch your mental forces to a new front: reviewing and perhaps adding to that list of possibilities.

Idea 34: Why consultation matters

It is rare for one person to see or understand all the feasible options in a given situation. That is why what the Romans called *consilium,* consultation, is so necessary before important decisions are taken.

Case study: Alfred Sloan

Alfred P. Sloan, a former head of General Motors, once said at a meeting of one of his top committees: 'Gentlemen, I take it we are all in complete agreement on the decision here?'

Everyone around the table nodded assent.

'Then,' continued Sloan, 'I propose we postpone further discussion of this matter until our next meeting to give ourselves time to develop disagreement and perhaps gain some understanding of what the decision is all about.'

Thorough discussion may throw up options that you did not initially consider. Even if that doesn't happen, all concerned will gain a better understanding of the pros and cons of each course of action. Everyone will have a proper understanding of 'what the decision is all about'.

Idea 35: Avoid an either/or mindset

When your enemy has only two options open to him you can be sure that he will choose the third.

Otto von Bismarck, Prussian statesman

The human tendency to dichotomize – to separate into two – is reflected in the way in which the word *alternative* (which means literally one or other of two things, the choice of one implying the rejection of the other) has come to be used instead of *possibility* (of which there can be many). We see life in terms of alternatives rather than possibilities, and are not aware that we are doing so.

Visualizing or recognizing a dichotomy because one is wearing mental blinkers must not be confused with the scanning process, whereby many courses of action or possible decisions are steadily reduced to a short list of two runners.

The either/or approach, especially when it becomes a mental habit, is dangerous because it oversimplifies reality. This may have been the fundamental flaw in the decision making of Adolf Hitler (after his abysmal set of values). Albert Speer, one of the Fuehrer's intimates, noted this trait: 'His close associates even openly made fun of Hitler, without his taking offence.' Thus his standard phrase, 'There are two possibilities,' would be used by one of his secretaries, in his presence, often in the most banal of contexts. She would say: 'There are two possibilities. Either it is going to rain or it is not going to rain.'

Experienced decision makers learn to be suspicious of premature consensus and either/or thinking. Peter Drucker declared provocatively: 'The first rule in decision making is that one does not make a decision unless there is disagreement.'

Wise leaders seek to proliferate courses of action. They keep the span of their attention widely focused, so that they receive the most light from the situation, before narrowing down the focus of their minds.

Idea 36: Using the lobster pot model

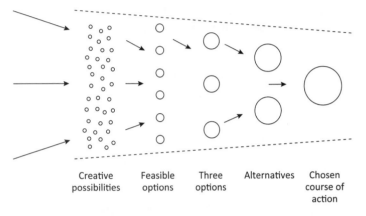

| Creative possibilities | Feasible options | Three options | Alternatives | Chosen course of action |

The lobster pot model

Possible is a very wide term, embracing everything that could be done within the limits of a particular situation, whereas *feasible* narrows it down a little to what can be done with existing resources.

The first thing to do is to sort out the *feasible* options from the greater number of *possible* options. Imagine yourself as a coin dealer or a diamond merchant sifting quickly through someone's collection and choosing the five or six specimens that are worth considering for purchase.

Then you need to proceed by *elimination*. Your aim is to reduce the feasible options to two alternatives – either this or that – as soon as possible. But remember the proverb: *More haste, less speed*.

The next step is to check if the alternatives are really mutually exclusive. After all, they may not have survived the mental obstacle course you have created for them unless you liked them both.

If, in fact, they are not attractive – if they are the two 'least worst' options – you may be pleased to drop one of them. But there are situations when you can opt for both of them, possibly in sequence – the 'trial-and-error' method, in which you can combine, mix or blend options in some other creative way.

Idea 37: Checklist – Options

Here are some useful questions to ask yourself and your colleagues when considering your options:

☐ Which possibilities are feasible, given our limitations?

☐ Which of the feasible options are the true alternatives?

☐ Are they mutually exclusive, or can we do
   Both, or
   Some creative combination of the two?

☐ Will the resulting compromise achieve our objective better than either of the discrete courses?

☐ Would it be better to do nothing?

☐ In what circumstances should we abandon the policy of keeping our options open for as long as possible?

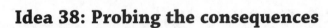

Idea 38: Probing the consequences

The whole process of making a decision can be summed up in three elements:

1. Making the decision.
2. Implementing it.
3. Living with the consequences.

It is helpful to bear in mind that consequences can be divided into six categories, which overlap considerably. These are described in the table below.

Probing the consequences

Type of consequence	Probing questions
Desirable	What solid advantages does this course or solution have in terms of the common purpose, aim or objective?
Undesirable	Does it have unwelcome side effects? Does it create more problems than it solves?
Manifest	What consequences – good or bad – are open to view now?
Latent	There will be consequences I cannot foresee now. Can I cut down their number by further thought or research? Have I sufficient resources to deal with possible contingencies?
Task	What are the technical consequences of adopting this method rather than that?
People	What will be the effects on (a) the team; (b) individuals; (c) the organization; (d) society; (e) myself?

In some instances you will be reduced to rough estimates or guesses about these consequences. But the greater the amount of science you bring to bear, the more you can predict the consequences with accuracy. Where possible, turn estimates into calculations. In industry that means carrying out a rigorous cost/benefit evaluation of the courses open to you.

Idea 39: The committee of sleep

It is a common experience that a problem difficult at night is resolved in the morning after the committee of sleep has worked upon it.

John Steinbeck, author of *The Grapes of Wrath*

Should you find the decision a difficult one, leave it for a while and then have another go at:

- ◆ Listing the advantages and disadvantages.
- ◆ Examining the consequences of each course of action.
- ◆ Measuring against standards, criteria and values.
- ◆ Testing beside the yardstick of the aim or objective.
- ◆ Weighing the risks against the expected gains.

Then try leaving the decision again for your depth mind to work on it. It is capable of processing information both consciously and unconsciously received over time.

With regard to 'people' consequences – a matter of vital concern to the leader – a common mistake is to guess the consequences instead of finding out by asking the people concerned. 'They will never agree to working extra shifts, that's for sure. They never have done in the past,' said a board director. But that is an unexamined assumption. Test that consequence to see if it is a real one – you may get a pleasant surprise.

The distinction between *manifest* and *latent* consequences is an important one, the former being those that are evident on examination, and the latter those that are unforeseen.

For example, it was not evident that the building of the Aswan Dam in Egypt would lead to the death of a certain species of fish in the Mediterranean (by cutting down the flow of fresh water into the sea).

Most decisions need correction to deal with such unforeseen or latent consequences, just as a car driver who corners to the right too soon has to turn the steering wheel over to the left to come back on course again.

Idea 40: Assessing risk

What makes decisions really difficult is the factor of high risk. You may recall the conflicting advice of the two proverbs *Look before you leap* and *He who hesitates is lost*.

There is an important skill in calculating risk. Calculation sounds mathematical, and there are plenty of management books with 'decision making' in the title that offer various 'probability theories' and statistical methods to take the pain out of risk assessment. Sometimes it can help to assign numbers and calculate in that way, but the contribution of mathematics to this field is very limited. Experience plays a much larger part.

One helpful idea is to define the worst downside: what happens in the worst scenario? Can you accept that, or will you be holed below the waterline so that the ship sinks? But in high-risk/high-reward situations, although you may know that you will be sunk if it does not all work out, you may still decide to take the high-risk course because the reward is just too important for you to forgo it.

You then have to address your mind to doing all you can to reduce the risk. It is here that experience, practice, consultation with specialists, reconnaissance and mental rehearsals may all be relevant techniques. You are trying to turn the *possibility* of success into the *probability* of success, but you will not be able to eliminate risk altogether: in this situation there are too many contingencies.

Whether or not it is right to proceed in any given situation where risk is present comes down to your experience and judgement.

You should always, however, bear in mind the wise words of Edward Whymper. After seven vain attempts he was the first to reach the summit of the Matterhorn in July 1865.

> *The line which separates the difficult from the dangerous is sometimes very shadowy, but it is not an imaginary line. It is a*

true line without breadth. It is often easy to pass, and very hard to see. It is sometimes passed unconsciously, and the consciousness that it has been passed is felt too late. If the doubtful line is crossed consciously, deliberately, one passes from doing that which is justifiable to that which is unjustifiable.

Idea 41: Consider your options

In the beginner's mind there are many possibilities, but in the expert's mind there are few.

Shunryu Suzuki, Zen Master

You need to open your mind into wide focus to consider all possibilities, and that is where creative thinking comes in. But then your valuing faculty must come into play to identify the feasible options – the ones that may or can be done, the practicable ones.

Notice the word *options* rather than *alternatives*. For an *alternative* is literally one of two courses open. Decision makers who lack skill tend to jump far too quickly to the either–or alternatives. They do not give enough time and mental energy to generating at least three or four possibilities.

When considering your options, remember that it tends to be easier to discard an option rather than to choose it. In other words, we are often better at knowing what we *don't* want to do rather than what we *do* want to do.

Remember to ask yourself whether or not you are overlooking some feasible course of action, perhaps because it is just too obvious. Always check your assumptions, for if they are faulty they can often rule out a feasible option. The less hidden they are, the better.

As a general principle, if you accumulate enough information you may not need to make a conscious decision. The decision will, as it were, be made for you. If there is no other feasible alternative it is comparatively easy to make up your mind what to do.

Case study: Why Athens became great

The great impediment of action is, in our opinion, not discussion but the want of that knowledge which is gained by discussion prior to action. For we have a peculiar power of thinking before we act too, whereas other men are courageous from ignorance but hesitate upon reflection.

Pericles, Athenian orator

Idea 42: The point of no return

Decision comes from the Latin words *de* and *caedere*, meaning 'to cut away'. It is related to such cutting words as 'scissors' and 'incision'.

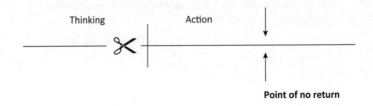

Point of no return

What is 'cut away' when you make a decision is the preliminary activity of thinking, especially the business of weighing up the pros and cons of the various courses of action. You now move into the action phase. Out with your cheque book – start talking about delivery dates! Things begin to happen.

It is always worth identifying what I call the Point of No Return (PNR), a term that comes from aviation. At the halfway point in crossing the Atlantic, it is easier for the pilot to continue to Paris in the event of engine trouble than to turn back to New York. The pilot has passed the PNR and is committed.

In its wider sense, the PNR is the point at which it costs you more in various coinages to turn back or change your mind than to continue with a decision that you now know to be an imperfect one.

In most decisions you do have a little leeway before you are finally committed: you can still change your mind. Often it is your depth mind that double checks the decision. It either whispers 'Yes, I am satisfied' or it begins an insidious and insistent campaign to make you at least review your decision, if not change your mind.

Responsibility for a decision includes responsibility for changing it up to the point of no return. This does not mean, however, that a decision that is adequate and able to achieve the aim should be abandoned because a better course of action suddenly presents itself.

Only if new factors weigh heavily against the feasibility of the adopted decision should another course be seriously considered. Once you are committed, beyond the no return point, new factors or proposals cannot by definition result in any change of course.

A corollary is that one should not commit oneself prematurely to a statement or position, as Alice found to her cost in *Through the Looking Glass.*

> 'The cause of lightning,' said Alice very decidedly, for she felt sure about this, 'is thunder – no, no!' she hastily corrected herself, 'I meant the other way.'
> 'It's too late to correct it,' said the Red Queen. 'When you've once said a thing, that fixes it, and you must take the consequences.'

The pressures to which the decision maker can be subjected (both from within and without) in the time between the act or moment of decision and the point of no return mount in ratio with the importance or gravity of the decision. The more costly an error, the more potential pressure the decision maker may experience, and the more they will need to be clear and firm in their judgement.

Often a leader's calmness and confidence, their ability to keep their head while others about them are, in Kipling's words, 'losing theirs and blaming it on him', will help to create the climate in which the decision can yet be effectively implemented, even though it may possibly not be the best one.

Once work has started on the plan, it may be necessary to revise or adapt the plan as circumstances or conditions dictate. Again, you must steer a middle course between the perennial need for flexibility as change unfolds and a certain persistence or tenacity in sticking to the agreed plan. Certainly, allowing too many unnecessary changes in the plan can itself breed confusion.

'As the military proverb says, "Order – counter-order – disorder."'

Idea 43: Practice makes perfect

To be good at anything at all requires a lot of practice, and to be really good at taking decisions you have to have plenty of practice at taking decisions.

Lord Thomson of Fleet, Canadian media entrepreneur

What the practice of decision making and the consequent experience does is to inform your depth mind so that it works much more quickly and more accurately. As Zen Master Shunryu Suzuki said, 'In the beginner's mind there are many possibilities, but in the expert's mind there are few.'

In his autobiography *After I was Sixty* (1975), Lord Thomson of Fleet wrote:

> *I cannot explain this scientifically, but I was entirely convinced that, through the years, in my brain as in a computer, I had stored details of the problems themselves, the decisions reached and the results obtained; everything was neatly filed away there for future use.*
>
> *Then, later, when a new problem arose, I would think it over and, if the answer was not immediately apparent, I would let it go for a while, and it was as if it went the rounds of the brain cells looking for guidance that could be retrieved, for by next morning, when I examined the problem again, more often than not the solution came up right away.*
>
> *That judgement seemed to be come to almost unconsciously, and my conviction is that during the time I was not consciously considering the problem, my subconscious had been turning it over and relating it to my memory; it had been held up to the*

light of the experiences I had had in past years, and the way through the difficulties became obvious.

Thomson added: 'This makes it all very easy, you may say. But, of course, it doesn't happen easily. That bank of experience from which I was able to draw in the later years was not easily funded.'

Idea 44: Depth minds at work

I know when I have a problem and have done all I can to figure it, I keep listening in a sort of inside silence until something clicks and I feel a right answer.

Conrad Hilton, founder of the Hilton Hotels chain

'Listening with the third ear', as it has been called, is a common characteristic of effective business leaders. It is a form of intuition, but whereas an intuition often comes unexpectedly, business leaders like Conrad Hilton expect their depth minds to work for them.

Case study: Conrad Hilton

Hotelier Conrad Hilton was once trying to buy an old hotel in Chicago whose owners promised to sell to the highest bidder. Several days before the deadline date for sealed bids, Hilton submitted a hastily made $165,000 offer. He went to bed that night feeling vaguely disturbed and woke the next morning with a hunch that his bid was not high enough. 'That didn't feel right to me,' he later wrote. 'Another figure kept coming, 180,000 dollars. It satisfied me. It seemed fair. It felt right. I changed my bid to the larger figure on that hunch. When they were opened the closest bid to mine was 179,000 dollars.'

Ask yourself
Can you think of a similar incident in your career so far where you have changed your decision based on a hunch?

By making a conscious effort to review your experience, you can develop your depth mind into a formidable instrument. Trusting it is important. You should also develop a special kind of inward sensitivity, so that you can pick up the delicate signals, the thought that stirs imperceptibly, like a leaf touched by the air, telling you that something is moving.

Idea 45: Five ways to improve your decisions

If one wants to be successful, one must think; one must think until it hurts. Believe me, that is hard work and, from my close observation, I can say that there are few people indeed who are prepared to perform this arduous and tiring work.'

Lord Thomson of Fleet, Canadian media entrepreneur

1. *The way to become good at decision making is to make lots of decisions in your field.*
   Practice makes perfect. That proverb will apply to decision making if practice is based on sound principles.
2. *See the relationships between your decisions, despite differences of time, place and scale.*
   Make connections between the problems you have faced in different contexts and those you encounter now. Those earlier decisions, correct or incorrect, are in your working memory.
3. *Look on your brain as a mental computer.*
   Earlier sequences of decisions and results are fed into the mind. Where solutions are not easily apparent, allow time for your depth mind to work on the problem. As a principle, a period of close enquiry and reflection should be followed either by a change of subject or a period of inactivity.
4. *Shun mental laziness.*
   At all stages of your career, conscious thinking demands some very hard work. You have to be prepared for that effort. If you do it when young you will reap the benefit of an exceptionally good depth mind.

5. *Few people are willing to make the effort.*

   That is a challenging comment. It could be good news for you. As the proverb says, 'The many fail, the one succeeds.'

Idea 46: Integrity in business decisions

Truth . . . is the sovereign good of human nature.

Francis Bacon, English philosopher and scientist

What the world needs is people who are both good leaders and leaders for good. What does 'good' mean in the context of business today? Why do some business decisions have the hallmark of integrity and others do not? The former chairman and chief executive of one of the world's ten largest companies once gave me this personal answer:

> *Most decisions in business are based on uncertainties because you don't have all the information you would theoretically like to have, but having what you have, you must use your judgement and decide.*
>
> *But, and this is what I mean by the overriding importance of integrity, the decision must be made within the framework of the responsibilities the business man carries. He has responsibilities to the shareholders, the employees, the consumer, even the government of the day. He has to balance these responsibilities thoroughly, justly and without bias.*
>
> *You could, for instance, make a decision which was to the benefit of your shareholders, but to the detriment of the community as a whole. Not doing that, and knowing why you are not going to do it, and what not doing it is going to cost you, is what I mean by integrity.*

Ask yourself
Do I agree with this definition of integrity?
Do the decisions of my company carry this hallmark?

Idea 47: The do nothing option

If none of the feasible options attract you and you cannot produce a satisfactory compromise, it is always worth asking yourself, 'Do I have to take action at all?' The option of doing nothing, of deciding *not* to act, is always worth considering. Sometimes the proposed cure promises to be worse than the disease.

However, the decision to do nothing must be taken for a very good reason and not because you cannot think of another way – still less because you are procrastinating or merely being indecisive.

An important principle to bear in mind is that problems often have a life cycle. Imagine that you are trying to manage two very difficult individuals, both recently transferred to you from other departments. Person A is young and has been with the company for only the graduate training 18 months; person B is due to retire at the end of next summer. Person A is at an early stage in the problem life cycle, so you must act. But person B is near the end of the problem life cycle: doing nothing (with damage limitation) is a real option.

> *'Sometimes it is wise to decide* not *to decide – to leave things as they are.'*

Idea 48: Banish the fear of mistakes

The fear of getting it wrong creates a climate in which anxiety, delay and indecision take root. Paradoxically, many books and courses on rational decision making, often replete with algebraic equations, can feed that fear of getting it wrong. You need confidence to make decisions. That means ridding yourself of the fear of making mistakes. Of course you will make mistakes, but that is better than doing nothing.

No manager in their right senses actually intends to make mistakes. They need a checklist to ensure that they remain in the flight path of the effective decision. Here are some key questions for your own checklist:

◆ Have I defined the objective?
◆ Do I have sufficient information?
◆ What are the feasible options?
◆ Have I evaluated them correctly?
◆ Does this decision feel right now that I have begun to implement it?

When you do make a mistake, turn your regrets into gold. Go back to your checklist and try to identify precisely where you went wrong. Then you will be learning by experience. That in turn will program your depth mind. Next time that red light will flash on sooner.

Nine Greatest Ideas for Sharing Decisions

Idea 49: Your role as leader

A key issue in leadership is how far the designated leader (appointed or elected) should share decisions with others, team members or colleagues. Of course, it is also an issue for all of us: how far should we make our decisions after solitary and silent thought, and how far should we consult others?

Before looking together at this decision-making aspect of leadership, let me put it into context by reminding you of the generic role of *leader*, which is true for all fields of work and all levels of leadership.

If you look closely at matters involving leadership, there are always three elements or variables:

1. *The leader* – qualities of personality and character.
2. *The situation* – partly constant, partly varying.
3. *The group* – the followers, their needs and values.

In fact, work groups are always different, just as individuals are. After coming together they soon develop a *group personality*. So that what works in one group may not work in another. All groups and organizations are unique.

Nevertheless, that is only half the truth. The other half is that work groups, like individuals, have certain needs in common. There are three areas of overlapping need that are centrally important, as illustrated in the diagram.

'*Always think* task, team *and* individual.'

Idea 50: Task, team and individual

Task need

Work groups and organizations come into being because there is a task to be done that is too big for one person. You can climb a hill or small mountain by yourself, but you cannot climb Mount Everest on your own – you need a team for that.

Why call it a need? Because pressure builds up a head of steam to accomplish the common task. People can feel very frustrated if they are prevented from doing so.

Team maintenance need

This is not so easy to perceive as the task need; as with an iceberg, much of the life of any group lies below the surface. The distinction that the task need concerns things, and the second need involves people, does not help much either.

Again, it is best to think of examples of groups that are threatened from without by forces aimed at their disintegration or from within by disruptive people or ideas. You can then see how they give priority to maintaining themselves against these external or internal pressures, sometimes showing great ingenuity in the process.

Many of the written or unwritten rules of the group are designed to promote this unity and to maintain cohesiveness at all costs. Those who rock the boat, or infringe group standards and corporate balance, may expect reactions varying from friendly indulgence to downright anger. Instinctively a common feeling exists that 'united we stand, divided we fall', that good relationships, desirable in themselves, are also essential means towards the shared end. I call this need to create and promote group cohesiveness the *team maintenance* need. After all, everyone knows what a team is.

Individual needs

Third, individuals bring to the group their own needs – not only the physical ones for food and shelter (which are largely catered for by the payment of wages these days), but also the psychological needs: recognition; a sense of doing something worthwhile; status; and the deeper need to give to and receive from other people in a working situation. These individual needs are perhaps more profound than we sometimes realize.

They spring from the depths of our common life as human beings. They may attract us to, or repel us from, any given group. Underlying them all is the fact that people need one another not only to survive but to achieve and develop personality.

Idea 51: The three circles interact

The three areas of need present in all working groups – task, team and individual – overlap and influence one another for good or for ill.

If the common task is achieved, for example, then that tends to build the team and to satisfy personal human needs in individuals. If there is a lack of cohesiveness in the team circle – a failure of team maintenance – then clearly performance in the task area will be impaired and the satisfaction of individual members reduced. Thus, we can visualize the needs present in work groups once again as three overlapping and interactive circles.

Nowadays when I show the model on a screen I usually colour the circles red, blue and green, since light (not pigment) refracts into these three primary colours. It is a way of suggesting that the three circles form a universal model. In whatever field you are, at whatever level of leadership – team leader, operational leader or strategic leader – there are three things that you should always be thinking about: *task, team* and *individual*.

The three-circle model is simple but not simplistic or superficial. Keeping in mind those three primary colours, we can make an analogy with what is happening when we watch a television programme: the full-colour moving pictures are made up of dots of those three primary and (in the overlapping areas) three secondary colours. It is only when you stand well back from the complex moving and talking picture of life at work that you begin to see the underlying pattern of the three circles. Of course, they are not always as balanced and clear as the model suggests, but they are nonetheless always there.

> **Ask yourself**
> Can you think of three examples where something that happened in one of the circles had symptoms or knock-on effects in the other two circles?

Idea 52: Eight functions of leadership

At whatever level of leadership we're considering, task, team and individual *needs* must be thought about continually. To achieve the common task, maintain teamwork and satisfy the individuals involved, certain functions have to be performed. A *function* is what leaders *do* as opposed to a *quality*, which is an aspect of what they *are*.

These functions (the *functional approach* to leadership, also called *action-centred leadership*) are:

1. Defining the task
2. Planning
3. Briefing
4. Controlling
5. Evaluating
6. Motivating
7. Organizing
8. Providing an example

Leadership functions in relation to task, team and individual can be represented by another three-circle model.

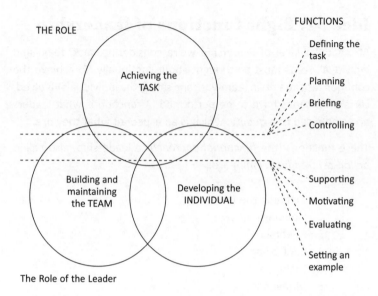

The Role of the Leader

These leadership functions need to be handled with excellence and this is achieved by performing them with increasing skill.

 Ask yourself
Which is my strongest function? And which is the function I most need to improve?

Idea 53: The decision-making continuum

If people are of one heart, even the yellow earth can become gold.

Chinese proverb

From the leadership perspective, the key issue is how far you should make the decision yourself or how far you should share it with your team. Let's look at the options.

Use of authority by the leader

Area of freedom for team members

1.	2.	3.	4.	5.	6.
Leader makes a decision and announces it	Leader 'sells' own decision	Leader presents ideas and invites questions	Leader presents tentative plan subject to change	Leader presents problem, gets suggestions, makes decision	Leader defines limits; asks team to make the decision

Decision Making Continuum

There is a lot to be said for moving as far to the right end of this continuum as you can. The key principle is that the more people share in decisions that affect their working life, the more they are motivated to carry them out.

That consideration, however, has to be balanced against the fact that the wider you open the door of the Inn of Decision, the less control you have of the outcome. The team may make a plan that, although it meets the boundary conditions or requirements you have specified, is not the way you would have done it yourself. Can you live with that?

Just where you should opt to decide on the continuum depends on several key factors, notably the time available and the competence level of the team members. There is no one right answer or 'style', as the academics used to call it.

The best leaders are consistent: you know where you stand with them and they are in many respects predictable. But when it comes to decision making they are infinitely flexible. So a good leader, working with individuals or teams, will operate at different points on the scale during a day.

Idea 54: The goal of consensus

I am a firm believer in the people. If given the truth, they can be depended upon to meet any national crisis. The great point is to give them the real facts.

US President Abraham Lincoln

Leadership is not solely about getting the intellectual quality of a decision right, important though this may be. It is about getting results through people. Therefore, the leader will need to include other people in the process of decision making. For a decision will be effective only if it is fully implemented. People are more likely to put their hearts into a decision if they have shared either explicitly or implicitly in the making of it.

People can participate in the early stages of the process, leaving the leader to take the final decision. They can, for example, contribute information or suggest a possible solution. How far a leader should go in sharing a decision with another person or a group depends on certain key factors: the kind of decision it is, the knowledge and experience of those concerned, and situational factors such as the time available for consultation.

Taking these factors into account there will be circumstances, especially as you rise up the promotion ladder, when you will want general agreement or consensus. Yet many managers are not clear what consensus means in this context. Here is a useful working definition:

When the feasible courses of action have been debated thoroughly by the group and everyone is prepared to accept that in the circumstances one particular solution is the best way forward, even though it might not be every person's preferred solution.

*The most important test is that everyone is prepared to act
as though it was their preferred course of action.*

Given a common commitment among group members to the purpose
and aims of the organization – a shared set of values – and an
absence of aggressive or arrogant egoism in individual group
members, consensus in the sense defined above is usually forthcom-
ing if time allows and you seek it with determination and skill.

Idea 55: How to achieve consensus

I have always endeavoured to listen to what each and every person in a discussion has to say before venturing my own opinion. Oftentimes, my own opinion will represent a consensus of what I heard in the discussion.

Nelson Mandela, South African statesman

Consent involves the will or the feelings and indicates compliance with what is requested, desired or necessary. In order to achieve the state of consensus in a group, time must be allowed for each member who wishes to speak to state an opinion – a personal judgement or belief falling short of positive knowledge – fully enough to get the feeling that others really do understand them.

This condition is necessary, otherwise a person who is speaking in opposition may justly harbour the feeling that their opinion would have been or should have been accepted if only the others had really listened and understood what they were saying. Only by all the group carefully listening to dissenting or opposing views can such feelings be nipped in the bud and effective group decisions eventually reached.

The end result – and the test – of consensus is commitment. And it is always actions, not words, that reveal commitment. Being able to argue one's case and yet to accept the final judgement of the common practical wisdom is the hallmark of both a good leader and a good team member.

Case study: Winston Churchill

Churchill was a persuader. Indeed, his skill in the use of words and logic was so great that on several occasions when he and I disagreed on some important matter – even when I was convinced of my own view and when the responsibility was clearly mine – I had a very hard time withstanding his arguments. More than once he forced me to re-examine my own premises, to convince myself again that I was right – or accept his solution. Yet if the decision went against him, he accepted it with good grace, and did everything in his power to support it with proper action. Leadership by persuasion and the wholehearted acceptance of a contrary decision are both fundamentals of democracy.

US President Dwight Eisenhower,
speaking of Winston Churchill

'Two heads are better than one.'

Idea 56: Checklist – Sharing decisions

☐ Have you agreed the aims and objectives with the team?

☐ Have you involved the team in collecting and sifting the relevant information?

☐ Has the team helped you to generate a number of possible courses of action?

☐ Have you used the synergy of the team members' minds to firm up the feasible options?

☐ Have you tested for consensus to see how far, in the circumstances, a course of action you favour is seen to be the optimum one?

☐ Have you secured everyone's commitment to make it work?

☐ Have you reviewed the decision with the team so that the lessons of success and failure are learned for the future?

Idea 57: The wisdom of groups

Three cobblers with their wits combined, equal Zhuge Liang the master mind.

Chinese proverb (Zhuge Liang, a famous statesman and strategist, was chief minister of the state of Shu 220–280 CE)

Thinking is both solitary and social. We need to think for ourselves – and make time to do so. But we also need to talk with and listen to others, for stimulus and encouragement, fresh perspectives and new ideas. Conversation at its best is a form of mutual thinking.

Outside the confines of the making of a particular decision you should always be open to the ideas, suggestions and information that people offer you. The more you show interest, the more that people will tell you, and you'll find that 10 per cent of their ideas are lined with gold.

The role of a leader is defined by the three circles of need – task, team and individual – and the corresponding set of functions. Communication and decision making are complementary dimensions. A key issue for all leaders is how far they should share decisions with their team or colleagues.

The more you share decisions, the higher the quality of the decision is likely to be. Moreover, the more people share decisions that directly affect their working life, the more they tend to be motivated to implement them.

Yet the exigency of the situation – shortage of time and the crisis factor – sometimes restricts the scope for sharing. And you also have to remember that the more you share a decision, the less control you have over that decision's quality and direction. So you need judgement here.

When the decision-making process is over, you will have to take the decision itself. Be decisive: show that the time for doubt and debate is over, and the time to plan, act and review is here.

Consensus leads to commitment, and commitment leads to all great human achievement.

When people are of one mind and heart, they can move Mount Tai.

Chinese proverb (Mount Tai in Shandong Province was the highest mountain known to Confucius)

Follow-up test

Decision-making strategies

- ☐ On a decisive–indecisive scale of 1–10, what number would best describe you?
- ☐ Can you recall all five steps in the decision-making process? If you had to alter the model, what new step would you add?
- ☐ Are you good at identifying the *relevant* factors in a decision-making situation?
- ☐ How would you distinguish between *manifest* and *latent* consequences?
- ☐ When making a decision, do you always identify and bear in mind the 'point of no return'?
- ☐ Have you ever made a decision that lacked the hallmark of integrity and lived to regret it?
- ☐ Are you free from the paralyzing fear of making a mistake but determined to do all in your power to avoid error if possible?

Sharing decisions

- ☐ Do you consult widely, and listen to the opinions or inputs of others, before taking a decision that directly or indirectly affects them?
- ☐ Where possible, do you work on the principle that the more people share in decisions, the more motivated they will be to carry them out?

☐ Before a meeting where a decision is to be taken, do you consider where on the decision-making continuum lies the most appropriate place for it to be taken?

☐ Do you 'own' the decision when you are consulting another person for their advice? Or does the other person 'own' the decision – it is their responsibility and they are accountable for it – where you are offering them your advice, knowledge or support?

PART THREE
How to Solve Problems

The world we have made as a result of the level of thinking thus far creates problems we cannot solve at the same level of thinking at which we created them.

Albert Einstein, German physicist

What decision making, problem solving and creative thinking all have in common is the fact that they are all forms of effective thinking. But there are some distinctions between them. You can, for example, think creatively, in the sense of having an original idea, without either making a decision or solving a problem. In Part Three the main focus is on problem solving.

Incidentally, we cannot imagine what it would be like to have no problems, can we? For to live is to have problems, and to solve problems, or find our way around them, is the great way in which our minds grow intellectually. If God had directly revealed his existence, the human mind would never have developed.

'Problems' sounds a rather negative term, conjuring up images of difficulty, frustration, unhappiness, even pain. Don't forget that opportunities are also benign problems: situations that challenge us and call forth a positive response.

Even those problems we all encounter that prove to be insoluble – unwelcome realities we can't alter or change – may one day come to be opportunities with thorns around them.

Eight Greatest Ideas for Problem-Solving Strategies

Idea 58: How solutions differ from decisions

Problem

Two girls and a woman want to sail to an island. Their boat holds either the two girls or the woman. If all are competent sailors, how can they get to the island in as few trips as possible?

Solution

Visualize that end state. If you work backwards from that first trip, you begin to see that someone has to bring the boat back from the island. Thus the two girls must sail over. One girl will remain on the island while the other sails the boat back. And the rest of the problem simply requires keeping track of where everyone is at a given time.

You will notice that in problems like these, all the elements of the solution are already there. All that you have to do is arrange or rearrange what has been given. In that sense, a problem is a solution in disguise.

As a result of solving such problems your life is not going to be different. By contrast, a decision usually *does* mean that life will be different. It opens the way to changes of some kind or other. Some of these changes are planned, wanted, expected or at least foreseen (the manifest consequences), whereas others are not. But solving or not solving the problem above – or any others like it – is not going to change your life in any way.

The English word 'problem' derives from the Greek *problema*, literally 'a thing thrown or put forward'. The second part of the word comes from a root that gives us also 'ball' and 'ballistics'.

Probably the earliest 'thing' thrown or put forward was a question for academic discussion or scholarly disputation, and the word has never quite lost an academic flavour owing to this parentage, as its frequent and specialized uses in the fields of logic, geometry, physics, mathematics and chess testify.

Academic problems tend to be presented in a theoretical way in a limited environment. In other words, the problem is put to you in such a way that it is capable of solution in terms of given (or easily acquired) information; there are clear limits around the problem, like a fence round a house. Its existence or solution does not really affect the environment in which it is presented. The solution of the problem is an end in itself, and not a means towards some other end.

Moving away from academic problems, puzzles and games, the problems we encounter in real life are mostly obstacles placed in front of us. If you decide to climb Mount Everest, for example, you may find that all goes well until, a day before your final ascent, a heavy storm suddenly develops on the South Col, the ridge leading to the summit. You have a problem!

Notice that you would not have that particular problem – or any problems – on Everest unless you had made a decision to climb to the summit. It is not a problem for anyone else. And it would cease to be a problem for you if you changed your mind and decided to go off and climb some other mountain in the Himalayas.

Therefore problems as obstacles or difficulties in the path ahead of us are always secondary to the results of decision making. Decisions create problems. One way of solving them – or rather the problem state in your mind – is to alter your decision, or at least your plan. Did you have a contingency plan, a Plan B for your route up the mountain if the weather deteriorated or avalanches (unexpected at this time of year) occurred? If you stick with your decision then, in consultation with your team, you have to find a way of overcoming the problem.

Why do we try to climb difficult mountains or invent perplexing puzzles and competitive games? Because there is nothing that humans enjoy more than solving problems. The skills of a problem solver in this limited sense, however, differ from those of a decision maker. As a problem solver you have to be clever, with analytical skills well honed by practice on many other problems in that particular field. By contrast, a decision maker needs a much wider range of skills and characteristics. You need to be intelligent, experienced and good.

> *'A problem is a solution in disguise.'*

Idea 59: A unisex model

He who would lead must be a bridge.

Welsh proverb

Because the mental approach you must use for problem solving is so similar to the decision-making process, a single model covering them both is possible. Think of it as a bridge spanning a river.

If you are trying to cross a mountain stream, you will jump from rock to rock, zigzagging your way to the far bank. Like thinking inside your head, this is an untidy but purposeful activity.

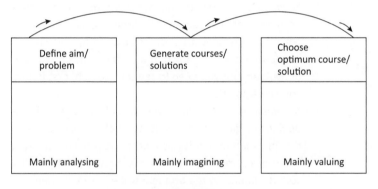

Crossing the river

However, when you have to get a team across a metaphorical river you need to be able to construct a simple bridge, so that everyone knows where they are in the decision making/problem-solving discussion.

You can see that the skills required change as one phase merges into the next. A new function with its family of more specific skills comes into play. The model is useful for your team as well as yourself. It can help everyone to keep in step.

Idea 60: Six steps for problem solvers

One should never impose one's views on a problem. One should rather study it, and in time a solution will reveal itself.

Albert Einstein, German physicist

You can develop your ability to exercise judgement soundly. Following the six steps below when you are confronted with a problem is a useful start. The resulting judgements, you may well find, are better than when you made no conscious effort to use your reasoning powers.

1. *Recognition* – General unease does not constitute a problem. There is something 'thrown forward' in one's path, a difficulty, obstruction or frustration, which has to be identified. Once known, the problem may be tackled or avoided, but you need to see the problem first before you see a solution.

2. *Accumulation of data* – Besides observation of the obvious or given data, this phase includes gathering all the information that is relevant to the problem at issue. The more complete the facts, the more likely it is that a sound solution to the problem will emerge. Remember, however, that drowning problems in an ocean of information is not the same as solving them.

3. *Classification and arrangement* – The third step is to classify or arrange the information into related groupings, which should throw light on a tentative answer.

4. *Formulation of a hypothesis* – Next, formulate a hypothesis or trial solution, one that in the light of the facts seems a likely answer.

5. *Corroboration* – The fifth step is to confirm or establish this hypothetical answer. Does it hold water? Does it

meet the requirements of a solution? Best of all, does it work in practice? The testing process to prove the answers may take some considerable time.

6. *Adoption* – The sixth step is the adoption or acceptance of the hypothesis or trial solution. Problem solved. You will need to monitor it, however, as the facts of the situation may suddenly or gradually alter. You should find that the results of applying the solution continue to be steadily satisfactory.

You may have noticed that this outline procedure is also the one you will have to follow if you plan to introduce a lasting change into the way an organization operates.

'Every problem contains within itself the seeds of its own solution.'

Idea 61: Checklist – Problem solving

A key skill, both when you are thinking something through by yourself and when you are leading or participating in a team, is to *ask the right questions*. Questions are the spanners that unlock the mind. Here are the kind of questions you should ask yourself – and others – during the process of tackling a problem.

Understanding the problem

☐ When did you first sense or become aware of the problem or the need for a decision?

☐ Have you defined the problem or objective in your own words? (Remember that a problem properly defined is a problem half-solved.)

☐ Are there any other possible definitions of the problem worth considering?

☐ Are you clear about what you are trying to do?

☐ Have you identified the important factors and salient facts? Do you need to spend more time on obtaining more information? Do you know the relevant policies, rules, limitations and procedures?

☐ Have you reduced the problem to its simplest terms without oversimplifying it?

Towards solving the problem

☐ Have you checked all your main assumptions?

☐ Out of all the possible courses or solutions, have you identified a short list of the feasible ones?

☐ Can you eliminate some of these in order to shorten the list still further?

Towards solving the problem

☐ If no solution or course of action seems right by itself, can you synthesize elements in two or more solutions to create an effective way of dealing with the problem?

☐ Have you clearly identified the criteria by which the feasible options must be judged?

☐ If you are still stuck, can you imagine yourself in the end state where you want to be? If so, can you work backwards from there to where you are now?

☐ Has anyone else faced this problem? How did they solve it?

Evaluating the solution and implementing it

☐ Have you used all the available information?

☐ Have you checked your solution from all angles and given it a test run?

☐ Are you clear about the evident consequences?

☐ Have you an implementation plan with dates or times for completion?

☐ Do you have a contingency plan if things do not work out as expected?

☐ When are you and your team planning to review the solution in the light of experience?

Idea 62: Reflecting on problems

To act is easy, to think is hard.

Johann Wolfgang von Goethe, German writer

People who are good with hammers see every problem as a nail! Make sure that you see the problem clearly and as it really is before applying any readymade solution. Whatever features the problem facing you may have in common with others, always be observant about what makes it unique.

Problems fall into two very broad categories: problems that are really obstacles of one kind or another that appear across your chosen path, and systems problems. If, for example, you change your course or plan, often problems of the first order simply disappear. If you decide not to climb Everest the snow blizzard ceases to be a problem.

The broad approach to both families of problems and to decision making is the same. Once again, it can be compared to building a bridge across a river resting on three pillars:

1. Defining the problem.
2. Generating feasible options.
3. Choosing the optimum course/solution.

A key thinking skill that you need to master is to ask the right questions – of yourself initially, but also of others. Questions are the spanners that unlock the problem in the mind, or at least the gates that bar entry to it. As the Chinese proverb says, 'A wise man's question is half the answer.'

Systems problems, as you will see in Idea 63, are best approached by regarding them as deviations from an expected norm. Diagnosis includes identifying and establishing the exact nature of that deviation and what caused it. The solution – if one is possible – is to remove the cause of the problem.

Few systems problems are completely intractable; you need the faith that they will eventually yield after a protracted siege from the human mind's analyzing faculty for logical thinking. You may not be the one to find the solution, but others will, for we build on each other's work.

If you find that a problem is really impossible to solve it may be a case of mistaken identity – it's not a problem, it's called *reality*.

Idea 63: How to tackle systems problems

Obstacle-type problems account for 80 per cent of the problems that leaders encounter, but you should also be aware of systems problems, the other 20 per cent. If you are a technical specialist, of course, those proportions are reversed and the majority of your working time will be spent on systems problems.

A system is a whole made up of integrated parts. It can be organic (your body), mechanical (your car engine) or a process (your system for billing customers). A systems problem is essentially a deviation from the norm. We can represent it visually by two lines, as in the diagram. The greater the difference between the normal performance (how the system is supposed to work) and the active performance (what is actually happening), the bigger the problem.

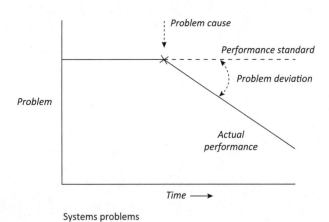

Systems problems

Dene the deviation

The main strategy for solving systems problems is to find the point of deviation and then establish what caused it. You need to find the exact time and place of that critical deviation. What happened? When? How much? Who was affected? Who saw it? And so on. Notice again that the key skill of asking the right questions is in play, focusing on the deviation point on the diagram.

Identify the cause or causes

Once you have pinpointed the deviation from the normal working of the system in question, list the possible causes. Now begin to eliminate the causes that can be proved innocent. You will be left with two or three suspects.

Case study: Plastec

Plastec, a company that made plastic containers, discovered that a rising percentage of its output was developing cracks. A project group studied the manufacturing process in detail and eventually defined the points of deviation: a change of supplier and a failure to clean out some storage vats. The new supplier inadvertently used these storage vats, and the plastic therefore became contaminated. Once the causes had been identified, the systems were altered to prevent any repetition, and the problem did not recur.

Beware of the fallacy of the single cause. In relatively simple problems there is only one cause, but in more complex ones two or three causes may be combining to produce the unwanted effect.

In Plastec's case it was the combination of two changes from the norm – a new supplier and poor cleaning procedures – that produced the problem.

Idea 64: Spot your problems early

One's objective should be to get it right, get it out, and get it over. You see, your problem won't improve with age.

Warren Buffett, US investor and philanthropist

'Walking around and talking to people helps me spot problems early,' one chief executive told me. 'Because I invest time in engaging people in casual conversation, they tend to point out potential problems I might not see otherwise.'

Do you make a practice of walking around and talking to your people?

The best thing you can do is prevent problems from arising in the first place. Identify the more vulnerable areas of your business. Spot the potential problems within each of these areas, together with their likely causes, and the actions you can take to prevent their occurrence.

If problems do occur anyway, make sure that you are ready to minimize the likely damage.

Know what your 'worst-case scenario' is and have a contingency plan in place to meet it. And then but only then – don't worry!

Case study: Napoleon at work

'I am used to thinking three or four months in advance about what I must do, and I calculate on the worst,' Napoleon explained to his brother Joseph. 'In war nothing is achieved except by calculations. Everything that is not soundly planned in its details yields no results.' He was not a man to leave things to chance.

'Plan for the unexpected.'

Idea 65: Face the cannons

The best way to escape from a problem is to solve it.

Welsh proverb

'Face the cannons,' Napoleon used to say to his soldiers. 'If the enemy is shooting at you, march towards them. If you turn and run from them, you'll get shot in the back.'

Not bad advice for any leader who is faced with a new and unpleasant problem, especially if it concerns people. Don't run away from it. Don't put your head in the sand. Don't delegate it – *deal* with it. If you lack the moral courage to do that, you shouldn't be in a leadership role. *Don't dodge problems but confront them.*

As a chief executive once told me:

> *Early in my career my initial reaction was to hesitate when faced with an uncomfortable situation. But over time I realized if you don't say 'no' early on to something you don't like – or if you don't face a problem head on and at an early stage – the issue will nag you. So you really have to learn to do just the opposite: confront the problem early and be honest with yourself when you're uncomfortable. Realize 'I'm not comfortable with the situation.' Find out why. Then give it your best shot to resolve the issue. It's important not to shirk an oncoming issue. Strip out the emotion, identify the problem, and do your best to tackle it immediately.*

What can you do to make the situation you face less difficult? Do it, even if you think you shouldn't have to do it.

'If you have to swallow a frog, do it quickly.'

Follow-up test

Problem-solving strategies

☐ 'Solutions are problems in disguise.' How far would you agree with this view?

☐ Are you clear in your mind about the distinction between problems as obstacles and systems problems?

☐ Do you spend as much time thinking about your opportunities as you do about your problems?

☐ 'Some problems get worse if you know the solution but procrastinate in implementing it.' Can you remember a time when you 'put off the evil day' and paid a price for doing so?

☐ Looking at the six steps of problem solving, can you from your experience add or subtract anything from that list?

☐ Can you think of a systems problem that you solved by following the rational step-by-step method?

☐ Do you tend to nip problems in the bud when they surface or delay dealing with them for as long as possible?

PART FOUR

Generating Ideas

An essential aspect of creativity is not being afraid to fail.
Edward Lane, British translator and lexicographer

In a decision-making or problem-solving situation, have you ever run out of ideas? If you have, then I know what that feels like!

Creative thinking and creativity can sometimes sound a little pretentious, but they do point to the remarkable capacity of our minds to generate new ideas. A traditional word for that faculty is *imagination*.

In Part Four we shall explore together some of the practical ways for developing your creative abilities so that you are never lost for an idea. Not to be without ideas is especially important if you are a leader. Most natural leaders are never short of them: it is their stock-in-trade. Leadership is about giving objective existence to desirable change, and creative ideas are the seeds of change.

They don't have to be *your* ideas. A key aspect of the art of leadership is being able to comb a team or an organization for the *best* ideas, and then putting them to work for the common good.

'Thinking is work', wrote the Canadian entrepreneur Lord Thomson. So it is, especially in the early stages of your career. But it is also fun. Fall in love with creative thinking – have fun!

Thirteen Greatest Ideas for Productive Thinking

Idea 66: Creativity

I know not what I may appear to the world, but to myself I appear to have been only like a boy playing on the seashore, and diverting myself in now and then finding a smoother pebble or a prettier shell than ordinary, whilst the great ocean of truth lay all undiscovered before me.

Isaac Newton, English scientist

Individuals clearly vary in their aptitude for creative work, and some psychologists have tried to distinguish the traits of the more creative thinkers. They come up with long lists of such qualities as intelligence, general knowledge, fluency, flexibility, originality, independence, scepticism, awareness, orientation to achievement, humour, psychological health, persistence, self-confidence, non-conformity, less-than-normal anxiety, dynamism and integration.

Such lists share the same disadvantages as those listing the traits of leaders: they do not agree with each other and tell us little that is peculiar to creative people, for there are many people who have some of the above qualities but are not particularly original. To say that creative people have 'originality' does not get us very far.

There is agreement, however, that certain conditions favour original or inventive thought. From my own studies of creative thinkers at work I have noticed the following tendencies:

♦ *Thinking is allowed to play with the materials at hand.* The mind is set in wide focus, and thus it observes or takes in what others would eliminate as irrelevant or accidental. Goals or problems, although of interest, do not dominate the foreground of the mind. There is a willingness to scrap the present goal or problem altogether if something more interesting (within the overall purpose) crops up. Here, the mind is like hanging sticky paper with which ideas collide like flies.

Examples

In 1822, the Danish physicist Oersted, at the end of a lecture, chanced to put a wire conducting an electric current near a magnet, which eventually led to Faraday's invention of the electric dynamo.

In 1889, Professors von Mering and Minowski were operating on a dog when an assistant noticed a swarm of flies being attracted to the dog's urine. He mentioned it to Minowski, who found that the urine contained sugar. This was the first step towards the control of diabetes.

In 1929, Sir Alexander Fleming noticed that a culture of bacteria had been accidentally contaminated by a mould. This led to his discovery of penicillin.

◆ *A prepared mind is important.* Besides the present data the depth mind is well stocked by background experience or reading in a variety of fields rather than any one speciality. As chemist Louis Pasteur famously wrote: 'Chance only favours invention for minds which are prepared for discoveries by patient study and persevering efforts.'

◆ *Conscious and unconscious thinking alternate.* There are periods of conscious work when the relationships between the material or information are analyzed as well as the question or problem being carefully formulated and perhaps reformulated several times. A problem well stated is a problem half solved.

◆ *One or more periods of depth mind activity occur.* Purposeful work is being done as if in a deep mine, out of sight and earshot.

Examples

Robert Louis Stevenson, like many other writers and artists, composers and inventors, was aware of the debt he owed to 'the little people, my Brownies, who do one-half of my work for me while I am fast asleep, and in all human likelihood do the rest for me as well, when I am wide awake and fondly suppose I do it for myself'. (In traditional stories a Brownie was a benevolent elf said to haunt houses and do housework secretly.)

The writer E.M. Forster used the metaphor of a deep well. 'In the creative state,' he wrote, 'a man is taken out of himself. He lets down as it were a bucket into his subconscious, and draws up something which is normally beyond his reach. He mixes this thing with his normal experience, and out of the mixture he makes a work of art.'

- ◆ *The depth mind is holistic.* There is a definite organic or holistic dimension in the way more creative minds work. It is revealed, among other ways, by a frequent use of the word *growth* in their accounts, and also a marked preference for organic metaphors and analogies. But this holistic attitude (to life as well as thinking) in creative people is complemented by rigorous analytical skills and the ability to judge one's own work. *Analyzing* and *valuing*, in other words, are as much at work as the *synthesizing* function of the mind.
- ◆ *Strong positive emotions accompany creativity.* Emotions or feelings precede, accompany and crown creative achievement. An outstanding thinker in any field is paid in the coinage of joy: a sudden overflow of excited feelings or a more lasting and quieter sense of profound fulfilment.

Example

After demonstrating the feasibility of protecting people against smallpox by vaccination, Edward Jenner wrote, 'The joy I felt at the prospect before me of being the instrument destined to take away from the world one of its greatest calamities . . . was so excessive that I sometimes found myself in a kind of reverie.'

Idea 67: Dots and matchsticks

Please solve the following two problems.

Problem 1: The nine dots

Take a piece of paper larger than this page and put on it a pattern of nine dots, like this:

•   •   •

•   •   •

•   •   •

Now, without taking your pen or pencil off the paper, connect up the dots by four straight consecutive lines. You should be able to complete this task within three minutes.

Problem 2: The six matchsticks

Place six matchsticks – preferably of the wooden variety – on a flat surface. Now arrange the matchsticks in a pattern of four equilateral (i.e. equal-sided) triangles. You may not break the matchsticks – that is the only rule.

Again, you should be able to complete this activity within three minutes. There are at least two solutions, but I am asking you for the most elegant one.

If you have been unable to solve the two problems, ask yourself why you are having such difficulty.

Let me give you a clue. The same principle that is preventing your mind from solving the problems is at work in both instances.

Still lost? Then turn to the Appendix for the explanation.

Idea 68: Always test your assumptions

To assume something is to take it for granted, to accept it as true without proof or as a hypothesis. An assumption is any assertion about reality that is unproved or debatable.

Conscious assumptions

Making an assumption –thinking or supposing *as if* something is the case – is a useful tool in argument or reasoning. It is the tentative adoption of an idea or interpretation, really for exploratory purposes. A hypothesis is a form of well-founded but tentative assumption. You are not committed to your hypothesis or assumption; you can jump off the bus any time you like.

Unconscious assumptions

Much more dangerous both to clear thinking and creative thinking, or to generating new ideas, are the unconscious assumptions that you may be harbouring in your depth mind. By definition, they are unexamined and, like land mines, they can have a devastating effect on your decisions.

Case study: How Hoover (UK) bungled a decision

A senior manager in the UK marketing department of Hoover, a household appliance company, once had the bright idea of introducing a 'free flights' promotional scheme as an incentive for buying its products.

It was a spectacularly bad decision. Some 200,000 people flew with the scheme, but it cost the company around £48 million. Another 127 people sought compensation in the courts, facing Hoover with a possible bill of millions of pounds if they succeeded. The president of Hoover Europe was dismissed from his £500,000-a-year post, and the US owners quickly sold the company for a knockdown price. You do not get decision making more wrong than that!

Why did this fiasco happen? Because the Hoover managers concerned made a false assumption. They assumed that when most of the people who bought appliances saw the small print wrapped around the 'free flights' offer – the complex restrictions and qualifications they deliberately built in to deter applicants – they would not bother to go through such a complex approach for the sake of a free air ticket.

But they underestimated the public! Enough people persevered in finding a route through all the complex rules and conditions that their free flights brought the company to its knees.

This true story is a parable to remind us of the importance of checking to ensure that we are not allowing unconscious assumptions to act like hidden reefs and rip the bottom of the ship.

Idea 69: Avoid negative critics

Ideas, especially when they are green shoots in your mind, are very vulnerable to the frost of negative criticism; later they may be able to take the strain. So avoid negative critics and let your ideas come to life.

Johann Schiller, a celebrated German poet who trained as a lawyer, then became a military surgeon and ended his career as professor of history at Jena in 1788, once wrote to a friend:

> *The reason for your complaint [about not being creative] lies, it seems to me, in the constraint which your intellect imposes upon your imagination. Here I will make an observation, and illustrate it by an allegory. Apparently, it is not good – and indeed it hinders the creative work of the mind – if the intellect examines too closely the ideas already pouring in, as it were, at the gates. Hence your complaints of unfruitfulness, for you reject too soon and discriminate too severely.*

The negative critic is like an underwater fisherman equipped with a gun and various darts, deadly phrases that he launches at any fish he sees stirring in your depth mind, such as:

- ◆ 'We tried that before.'
- ◆ 'Let's get back to reality.'
- ◆ 'I don't like the idea.'
- ◆ 'Good idea in theory – but impracticable.'
- ◆ 'You'll make us a laughing stock.'
- ◆ 'Where did you dig that one up from?'
- ◆ 'It's never been tried before.'
- ◆ 'It won't work here.'
- ◆ 'It can't be done.'
- ◆ 'We've always done it this way.'
- ◆ 'It costs too much.'

A true or constructive critic, however, might be defined as one who expresses a reasoned opinion on any matter involving a judgement of its value, such as truth, beauty or technical quality.

That critic appreciates the value that exists. The constructive part comes into play when such a critic suggests ways in which value can be added to the idea or matter under scrutiny. They build on your ideas.

When it comes to trying to think about fresh possibilities, there are two kinds of people. The first, when confronted with a new idea, will react in a distinctly negative way. By clear, logical thinking they may soon be able to show that the idea is wrong or that the plan is unworkable. The second type will react differently. They will toy with it, and speculate what the implications might be if the idea could be put into practice. Because of the novelty of the proposal, their impulse is to wish it could be shown to be true.

A condition of creativity seems to be a readiness to side with, empathize with, and explore the possibilities of fresh ideas. It also seems to be compatible with the attitude of discriminating criticism previously discussed. The attitude consists, in fact, of vigorous attention to ideas which, because they are important, merit criticism in the interests of their refinement or extension.

Make the overmighty analyzers wait their turn. Let your mind off its habitual leash so that it roams freely wherever it wills to go in the field you have chosen.

Idea 70: Holistic thinking

I can see the whole of it at a single glance in my mind, as if it were a beautiful painting or a handsome human being.

Wolfgang Amadeus Mozart, German composer

A holistic mind is diametrically opposed to an analytical mind. The latter separates wholes into their constituent parts. That works well with inanimate objects, but not with living beings. Then, As Wordsworth said, 'we murder to dissect'.

In contrast, knowing how to think holistically, to see the wood as well as the trees, to see the whole that is a sum of more than the constituent parts, is a key skill for an effective thinker.

Those who have good judgement of people tend to have more holistic minds. People may have sets of qualities or strengths and weaknesses, but a psychological analysis of their traits seldom gives you a sense of knowing them. You are always dealing with a whole person.

Holistic minds tend to be attracted to growth. They like to help individuals and teams, organizations and communities, even nations, grow to their full potential.

Are you holistically minded? Here is a simple test. If you are trying to understand a complex social situation, do you prefer someone to analyze it for you? Or is the gateway of understanding for you the story of how the situation developed? Holistic people like to know the story behind a person or situation.

Ask yourself
How can I strengthen my ability to think holistically about people and problems?

Idea 71: The holistic mind at work

In 1927 Field Marshal Jan Smuts, a keen agricultural scientist as well as a soldier and statesman, published a book entitled *Holism and Evolution*. *Holism* was the word he coined to describe the tendency in nature to produce wholes by ordering or grouping various units together.

The essential realities in nature, so Smuts wrote, are these irreducible wholes. They cannot be analyzed into their parts without losing this holistic quality. His neologisms – holism and holistic – subsequently entered the English language.

Anybody who has responsibility for the affairs of an organization, whether their title is chief executive, general manager, president or managing director, has to take a holistic view of it. Indeed, holistic thinking is the key to strategic thinking in any field.

Systems as holistic concepts

Another word that has worked well as a label for this box of mental attitudes and faculties is *system*. We are surrounded by systems, wholes that are made up of interacting parts while somehow transcending them.

Look at a candle flame. Why does it keep at approximately the same size and shape while it's flickering? In this case, the 'parts' are flows of vaporized wax, oxygen and burnt gases. The processes of combustion and diffusion give the interactions between these flows, and these interactions show us at what size and shape the flame will be approximately stable.

The strength of a rope is another example of a holistic property. This strength is a result of interaction among the individual strands, caused by twisting. With the strands untwisted, the rope's strength is governed by the weakest strand; twisted, the strands act together and increase their strength.

A holistic mind therefore has a special way of looking at things or people, at the world itself. It is not eager to take things to bits at first glance. Rather, it waits to see the full pattern, the whole – the wood rather than the trees. Equal mental weight is given to the whole in relation to the parts, hence there is a certain reluctance to dismember it. If a cruel schoolboy pulls the legs and wings off a fly he is left with a dead fly: the parts are there but the whole is gone.

Thinkers such as Einstein exemplify this union of formidable powers of analysis with a strain of holistic thinking that seeks out the simple or the whole.

Werner Heisenberg, one of the fathers of quantum physics, once spoke to Einstein of the 'almost frightening simplicity and wholeness of the relationships which nature suddenly spreads out before us'.

This theme of simplicity, wholeness and beauty, revealed through mathematical formulae or detailed experimentation, recurs again and again as nature's mysteries are explored.

There is definitely a family relationship between imagination and holistic thinking. Take as an example this description of the crucial phase in composition by one of the world's great composers, Wolfgang Amadeus Mozart. I have put key words in **bold** to emphasize the proximity of the two concepts of holistic and imaginative work in this particular passage:

> First bits and crumbs of the piece come and gradually join together in my mind; then the soul getting warmed to the work, the thing **grows** more and more, and I spread it out broader and clearer, and at last it gets almost finished in my head, even when it is a long piece, so that I can see the **whole** of it at a single glance in my mind, as if it were a beautiful painting or a

*handsome human being; in which way I do not hear it in my imagination at all as a succession – the way it must come later – but all at once as it were. It is a rare feast. All the **inventing** and **making** goes on in me as in a beautiful strong dream. But the best of all is the hearing of it all at once.*

> *'A whole is more than the sum of its parts.'*

Idea 72: Ideas grow like plants

So nature, wholeness and growth are all key ideas for the holistic mind. Far from being an artificial or manmade activity, synthesis is the central natural process. Breaking down wholes into their parts – that decaying tree trunk in our garden – are only preludes to a series of syntheses.

When we synthesize consciously, putting together elements into a compound, we are only palely imitating what nature is doing all the time. Because we are part of nature, however, that natural process of growth can happen inside our minds as well as our bodies. *Ideas can start as seeds and then grow.*

This notion of ideas growing is important to holistic thinkers and may make them reluctant to submit ideas to early analysis by themselves or others. A newborn baby is a whole. It grows. But in the first days of its life it needs protection from the chill winds.

Another related distinguishing characteristic of holistic thinkers is that they make considerable use of the *story* as their principal route to understanding another person or a situation, rather than breaking the analysis into separate parts. They like to know how something began and how it developed.

Holistic thinking, then, is as relevant to the manager as it is to the artist, doctor or scientist. The capacity to think about organizations and teams, opportunities and problems as wholes is extremely important. You can even think holistically about a budget or a balance sheet if you are gifted that way.

Would you say you are a holistic thinker? You can certainly develop holistic thinking by becoming more aware of its importance and by deliberately refraining from analysis beyond a certain point. Let the whole take shape in your mind's eye.

Idea 73: Imaginative thinking

> *As a rule grown-up people are fairly correct on matters of fact;*
> *it is the higher gift of imagination that they are so sadly to seek.*
>
> Kenneth Grahame, author of *The Wind in the Willows*

Successful chief executives rate imagination high on the list of attributes they value most (see Idea 14, where it is listed in fifth place out of 25 desirable attributes). But what is imagination and how does it contribute to business success? Here is British businessman Lord Sainsbury's evaluation:

> *The characteristic in a good manager which I appreciate almost above all else is that of the imagination. The good manager has to be imaginative in order to be a successful innovator. Success in that respect brings not only a valuable contribution to any enterprise, but also the considerable personal satisfaction of creative achievement.*
>
> *It is imagination that is needed to anticipate events and to respond to change. It is only those with a lively imagination who can really develop sensitive understanding of others, be they customers, colleagues or shop floor workers. To be able to do that is a vital ingredient of success in commerce or industry.*

Our minds have a fundamental visual capacity: we not only see things but we can shut our eyes and remember the picture of what we have seen.

It is useful to bear in mind the pictorial dimension of imagination but, beyond a certain point, it is better to use the word in a much broader sense. Avoid getting too hooked on trying to see or make mental pictures: you can think imaginatively without them. Equally, you can imagine without thinking.

A mother, anxious when her child has not come home from school, imagines all sorts of scenes. She is the passive prey of horrible fantasies, which come into her mind successively in a way she cannot control. Emotion and imagination have joined forces. Her imagination is hyperactive and her powers of thinking unexercised. She is panic stricken. In this situation thought and imagination are diametrically opposed.

In other situations we are inclined to distinguish thought and imagination as merely different. For example, if you read a scientific account of the geography of northern Greenland, you might be thinking analytically about the climate, flora and fauna, whilst also trying to visualize what the country looks like and what life might be like there. You will be thinking like a physical geographer while also composing a scenario for yourself in your imagination.

But there is a group of situations in which a person's thinking and imagination are really inseparable, and in which the thinking is imaginative. Take a good detective or a top-class manager. In trying to work out problems they need to be both fertile in imagining feasible hypotheses and also careful about their data and what can be properly deduced. They must think imaginatively, but also in a coherent, methodical and unfanciful way.

We find it hard to rid ourselves of the assumption that imagination is exercised only in dreaming up fictional things or happenings. William Shakespeare declared that 'imagination bodies forth the forms of things unknown'. He did invent a living world of fictional characters and incidents. But Leonardo da Vinci and Thomas Edison had good imaginations too. Prospero and Hamlet are imaginary people, but the submarine and helicopter, the electric light bulb and the telephone are not imaginary objects, though it needed a combination of imagination and technical knowledge to invent them.

Idea 74: Imaginative abilities of the mind

Imagination is more important than knowledge. For while knowledge defines all we currently know and understand, imagination points to all we might yet discover and create.

Albert Einstein, German physicist

The human mind has a remarkable range of imaginative abilities, from memory function at one end of the scale to creative imagination at the other.

Recalling	The ability to bring a picture back to mind, something not actually present to the senses, such as your house or car.
Visualizing	The ability to form a picture of something not experienced in its entirety, such as what it would be like for you to walk on the moon.
Creating	The ability to form an image or whole of something actually non-existent at present, such as a new product.
Foreseeing	The ability to see a development or outcome before it materializes.
Fantasy	The ability to invent the novel and the unreal by altering or combining the elements of reality in a particularly unrestrained and extravagant way.

Ask yourself
Does your imagination have real thrust and life? Can it get you off the runway of perceived reality?

Idea 75: Exercise your imagination

Situation 1

Imagine you are climbing Everest by yourself and without oxygen. You are 1,000 metres from the summit.

(a) Sit down and make a meal for yourself. Work through each of your five senses to complete the scene in your mind.

(b) You are now pressing on to the summit. What can you see? What are you touching? What are your feelings? What colours can you see?

(c) Now you are on the summit. You have a camera with you. Set it up on a rock. Stand back. Now compose in detail the photograph you have taken. Turn it into a three-dimensional picture.

Situation 2

A new creature has been discovered in the jungles of South America that is destined to replace the dog and the cat as our most popular domestic pet. Briefly describe it in 200 words and draw a picture of it. Give it a name.

Situation 3

Morwenstow is a small village on the north coast of Cornwall. One Sunday evening during the Napoleonic Wars, the vicar was preaching at evensong in the village church. A great storm raged outside. Suddenly the congregation heard a great crash. A vessel had struck the rocks. Everyone rushed out of the church and with the vicar at their head they hurried down the steep path to the bay. In the dusk they saw the smashed wreck of a three-masted schooner, its debris scattered on the beach. There was apparently only one survivor lying unconscious on the sand. He was a swarthy man, dressed in a sea captain's uniform. But when they turned him over a look of terror came over the vicar's face . . .

Now continue the story.

> *Use it or lose it.*
>
> Modern proverb

Successful generals down the ages have shown the capacity to think imaginatively. Winston Churchill once wrote:

> *Nearly all the battles which are regarded as the masterpieces of the military art have been battles of manoeuvre in which very often the enemy has found himself defeated by some novel device, some unexpected thrust or strategy. In such battles the losses of the victor have been small and the enemy is left puzzled as well as beaten.*

In business your next move is not blueprinted for you. It's true, you don't have total freedom. You don't have the freedom of, say, someone writing a television script or the composer of a poem. But you are like a person crossing an unmapped plateau.

You have to think up for yourself and then experimentally try out possible ways of getting where you want to be – and the solutions to these problems are not in books, nor can they be recalled from your memory bank. For you have never been here before. You have to originate or innovate, and you cannot innovate by following established precedents or by applying common recipes. That is why imagination is so important for you as a leader and a manager.

Idea 76: Imagination in action

Imaginative thinking is not limited to inventions. The detective and the manager are usually not inventing or making anything, but they are still thinking imaginatively. They are also linked in that they both have an adversary: the criminal in one case and competitors in another. Sportspeople and soldiers share that factor as well.

Again, let's look at an example. When a famous football player is being praised for playing imaginatively, he is not being praised for fantasizing in his armchair or writing novels about football. Rather, he is seen to do things such as the following:

♦ In trying to get past the opposing player he doesn't use the same move or swerve time after time – or he may do so three times just in order to surprise his opponent on the fourth occasion with a change of direction.
♦ He doesn't assume that his team mate will pass out to the right, as he did the last five times – he is ready for the ball to come to him this time.
♦ He quickly realizes that a gap is likely to open up where, at the moment, no gap can be seen.

In other words, he is quick to anticipate, to see and to act on things that are out of the ordinary. He surprises his opponents and yet he is not taken by surprise. He exploits the unexpected and the lack of routine.

This imaginative thinking on the football field has nothing to do with whether or not the player concerned writes fictional stories about football. It also has nothing to do with the rational and logical thinking prized so highly by academics. Ron Greenwood, a former manager of the England football team, once said that 'football is a battle of wits' for which a combination of physical and mental attributes is needed:

A football brain is quite different from an academic brain. I coached at Oxford University for seven years and if the students had had the right kinds of football brains they would have been the best team in the world. But they didn't and they weren't. A man who can hardly read or write can have a great football brain.

Idea 77: Imagination in perspective

Imagination should not be promoted to top place in the hierarchy of thinking abilities. It should be a team player, not the captain. It is the vanguard, the advance scouting party, of thinking. The specific role of imagination is to lead us into innovating, inventing, creating, exploring, risk taking and adventuring.

The leader who knowingly ventures off or beyond the beaten track, the path of well-trodden expectations, is showing some degree of imagination. Their business ventures may turn out to be fruitless, random or crazy, nevertheless. For leaders who dream, dreams may be pathfinders, but they may also lead to the bankruptcy courts. Of those who depart from well-established ways only a few are explorers. 'Imaginative', 'inventive' and 'adventurous' are terms of praise, but equally 'fanciful', 'reckless' and 'crazy' describe those who are failed imaginative thinkers.

Be on your guard, therefore, against any tendency to glorify the notion of imagination as an end in itself. People sometimes forget that a lively imagination can also be a silly one. Scope for originality is also freedom to be a crackpot. Both the genius and the crank are imaginative thinkers – some are both at the same time.

Yet imagination covers some crucial qualities in the business leader. There will be plenty of situations in your future career that will call on your powers of originating, inventing, improvising, discovering, innovating, exploring, experimenting and knowingly leaving the beaten track. Can you imagine yourself now doing all those things?

Ask yourself

Do you see yourself as having an analytical mind that is sometimes imaginative, or an imaginative mind that is also analytical?

When you visualize yourself – the concept you have of yourself – do you see or sense considerable potential waiting to be realized inside you?

Imagine yourself in five years' time as a chief executive with a proven reputation for imaginative action. How did you acquire that reputation? Create three more or less credible fantasies to explain your sudden emergence from the pack.

Idea 78: Checklist – How imaginative are you?

□ Can you recall visually with great accuracy? Imagine your last holiday and see how much detail you can see in the mental pictures.

□ Would you describe yourself as good at visualizing things you haven't directly experienced yourself? Could you, for example, accurately imagine what it would be like to be a member of the opposite sex? Or prime minister?

□ Or your assistant?

□ Has anyone praised you for your imagination within the last year?

□ Have you invented or made anything recently, at work or in your leisure time, that definitely required imagination?

□ Do you tend to foresee accurately what happens before the event?

□ Do you daydream about your work or career?

□ Do you paint or draw?

□ Do you find it easy to choose colour schemes when you have to redecorate?

□ Do you find that you can think up names for babies, pets, houses?

□ Have you ever written a story or a poem?

Eleven Greatest Ideas for Useful Originality

Idea 79: Quantity or quality?

To create is always to do something new.

Martin Luther King, US civil rights activist

New ideas are essential for industry, commerce and the public sector alike. Innovative products and different ways of doing things are the lifeblood of successful enterprise.

We all have new ideas. We vary, however, in terms of the *quantity* we produce in our lifetime, and still more in the *quality* of those ideas. People who have many new ideas with a high rate of excellent ones among them are the ones we tend to call creative thinkers.

High	**A** High productivity and few quality ideas	**C** Many quality ideas with high productivity
PRODUCTIVITY OF IDEAS	**B** Not very productive and not producing many 'pearls'	**D** Many quality ideas with low productivity
Low	QUALITY OF IDEAS	High

Creativity ratios

Case study: Dr R. Buckminster Fuller

An example of an A-type thinker is Dr R. Buckminster Fuller, an inventor, engineer, architect-designer and philosopher. After being expelled from Harvard and failing as a businessman, he turned to architecture and invention.

One of the most controversial architectural figures of our time, he produced designs for unprecedented types of structure that reflected his belief and optimism in the benefits of modern technology. Thus his Dymaxion House of 1927 saw the modern home not in terms of a walled structure but as technology servicing the human life within it. The house hung from a mast on a wire construction. The Dymaxion three-wheeled car of 1932 similarly rejected the traditional coach maker's craft to produce a futuristic design.

However, none of Fuller's inventions caught on before he conceived the Geodesic Dome, a linking of triangles into a strong and lightweight sphere. It was another result of his relentless pursuit of architectural forms along the path of mathematical logic. Architects hailed it as a genuine advance and Fuller's public image as a lovable crackpot began to change. Unlike classic domes, his did not depend on heavy vaults or flying buttresses for support. The weight load was transmitted throughout the structure, producing a high strength-to-weight ratio. More than 3,000,000 domes have since been built.

The word 'creative' should be bestowed rarely. It always implies a value judgement. A good idea is one that a critical mass of people deem to be both useful and original.

Therefore we should separate in our minds the two dimensions of creativity: quantity and quality. There are prolific novelists in most countries but we can all probably think of a writer who produced only a few works of real genius.

Creativity is a holistic combination of mental abilities and qualities of personality, temperament and character. At the heart of that combination, however, is synthesizing: the ability to combine miscellaneous things into new wholes.

Idea 80: The creative thinking process

The intellect has little to do on the road to discovery. There comes a leap in consciousness, call it intuition or what you will, and the solution comes to you and you don't know how or why.

Albert Einstein, German physicist

Creative thinking can be seen as having four phases:

Preparation	The hard work. You have to collect and sort the relevant information, analyze the problem as thoroughly as you can, and explore possible solutions.
Incubation	This is the depth mind phase. Sitting on eggs until the young birds of ideas emerge is a metaphor for the depth mind's work. We all have a purposive and helpful depth mind; we differ as to the use we make of it. Mental work – analyzing, synthesizing and valuing – continues on the problem in your subconscious mind. The parts of the problem separate and new combinations occur. These may involve other ingredients stored away in your memory.
Insight	The 'Eureka' moment. A new idea emerges into your conscious mind, either gradually or suddenly, like a fish flashing out of the water. These moments often occur when you are not thinking about the problem but are in a relaxed frame of mind.
Validation	This is where your valuing faculty comes into play. A new idea, insight, intuition, hunch or solution needs to be thoroughly tested. This is especially so if it is to form the basis for action of any kind.

Although it is useful for you to have this framework in mind, remember that the actual mental process is a lot more untidy than this list suggests.

Remind yourself

Think of the phases as being four notes on a piano that can be played in different sequences or combined in complex chords.

Idea 81: Creativity in action
– Thomas Edison

> *A successful man is a friend to failure.*
>
> Chinese proverb

Continually called a genius himself, Thomas Edison gave some thought to what the word meant, coming up with the famous definition: 'Genius is 1 per cent inspiration and 99 per cent perspiration.' He enlarged on this to his secretary:

> *Well, about ninety-nine per cent of it is a knowledge of the things that will not work. The other one per cent may be genius, but the only way that I know to accomplish anything is everlastingly to keep working with patient observation.*

Even with Edison's phenomenal work rate, however, it is unlikely that most of us would come up with even one invention of the calibre of the light bulb in the course of a lifetime. He invented not only the light bulb but the phonograph, the telephone (concurrently in competition with Bell), the means of distributing electrical power, X-ray plates and so on until the very end of his life.

The capacity of the man is almost unimaginable. He was able to conceive of machines for recording what we hear, which turned out to be the phonograph, and for recording what we see, which became the moving camera, both of which were outside the realm of anything existing then, so that their conceptualization was a supreme work of imagination.

Confronted with a problem, Edison was able to see how the solution might be arrived at. He could imagine, in the broadest terms, the short and long-term consequences of his inventions. And all that lay between him and these goals was a great deal of hard work, which he could not wait to dispose of as soon as possible.

Edison's life was ruled by the excitement of the hunt. He once said to a colleague:

> *I don't think Nature would be so unkind as to withhold the secret of a good storage battery if a real earnest hunt for it is made. I'm going to hunt.*

And hunt he did, whether for the secret of the battery, the right filament for the incandescent bulb, the best mixture for insulating cables, or whatever the current problem might have been in the most methodical and exhaustive manner.

There was never any time to spare; as soon as one problem was solved, another idea was waiting to be put to the test. There was never enough time – and he knew there was not – to investigate all his ideas.

For example, it was not in the end Edison but the Wright brothers who made a successful aeroplane, although as early as 1889 Edison told a journalist:

> *You can make up your mind . . . that these fellows who are fooling around with gasbags are wasting their time. The thing can't be done on those lines. You've got to have a machine heavier than air and then find something to lift it with. That's the trouble, though, to find the 'something'. I may find it one of these days.*

Ask yourself
What are the three key lessons I can learn from Edison's productive life?

Idea 82: Widen your span of relevance

It is the function of creative people to perceive the relations between thoughts, or things, or forms of expression that may seem utterly different, and to be able to combine them into some new forms – the power to connect the seemingly unconnected.

William Plomer, English poet

For most of us, *relevance* means having a relation to or a bearing on the matter in hand or the present circumstances. In discussion, for example, a *relevant* comment, suggestion or idea has a traceable connection, especially a logical connection, with whatever is under consideration. Therefore it has significance in some degree for those who are engaged in such consideration.

In a court of law it is the judge's responsibility to determine what is relevant to the case and what is not. Relatively speaking, when it comes to evidence the judge has a narrow span of relevance. When it comes to precedents, however, the best judges have a much wider span of relevance: they can connect the issues in this case with a dozen others down the centuries.

Creative thinkers tend also to have a wide span of relevance. In particular they can see similarities or analogies between things that appear to other people to be completely separate and therefore *irrelevant* phenomena. The classic example is the inventor who sees the relevance of a given technology in one field to a problem in another quite remote field.

Case study: Jethro Tull

Called 'the greatest individual improver that British agriculture had ever known', Tull was by origin a musician and a lawyer and he went into farming out of necessity.

Before, his time sowing was done by means of a wheeled vehicle that held the seed in a container; as the wheels turned the seed ran down through metal tubes or hollowed coulters underneath. The front of each coulter made a small furrow in the soil and the seed ran into it. A bush harrow drawn behind the drill restored the soil and covered the seed.

Earlier seed-dispersing machines had failed because they could not effectively control the flow of seed from container to soil. Tull, a musician, solved the problem by adapting the mechanism on the sounding board of a church organ to the seed drill he was making. He controlled the flow of the grain by means of a brass cover and adjustable spring, copied from the tongue in the organ mechanism.

Exercise

List specific inventions or developments that were (or might have been) suggested to creative thinkers by the following natural phenomena. Turn to the Appendix for the answers.

1. Human arms
2. Cats
3. Seagulls
4. A frozen salmon
5. Spiders
6. Earthworms
7. A flower
8. The eye of a fly
9. Conical shells
10. Animal bone structures

Remind yourself

Interest, observations, storage in memory and synthesis are the key constituents of creative thinking. A wide span of analogy is essential.

'The most original person is the one who borrows from the most sources.'

Idea 83: Make fuller use of your depth mind

To raise new questions, new possibilities, to regard old problems from a new angle, requires creative imagination.

Albert Einstein, German physicist

Synthesis of apparently unrelated things or ideas carried out at the conscious level is not the same as free-range, natural creative thinking. In the latter the process of synthesis takes place at a less than conscious level.

The poet C. Day Lewis once described the process in a lecture thus:

> *What seems to happen for a poet is that experience sinks down on to the seabed of the unconscious. And lying there for a length of time, it is changed: 'those are pearls that were his eyes'.*
>
> *And one day a fragment of this buried treasure floats to the surface. It comes to me, very often, in an enigmatic form – a form of words, a brief phrase, which is attended by a special feeling of anticipation, excitement. It comes, more often than not, quite unexpectedly, when the mind is in neutral, or thinking of something else.*

You can see the depth mind principle at work, but with much more emphasis on a holistic or growing synthesis – the conception of an idea followed by a period of gestation in the womb of the mind.

Scores of people have made creative breakthroughs by programming their mind and letting the purposeful unconscious part of it work for them. When they have ceased straining for the answer it arrives in a flash, out of the blue, or as a hunch, while they are relaxing by doing something with their hands or body.

A British Nobel prize winner, Dr Godfrey Hounsfield, made the crucial breakthrough that led to the development of the MRI (magnetic resonance imaging) body scanner while indulging in his favourite hobby, rambling. 'I'm very keen on rambling,' he said later. 'It's a time when things come to one, I find. The seeds of what happened came on a ramble.'

Learning to relax and listen for the answer is a necessary condition for creative thinking. Times just before going to sleep or shortly after awaking, when the body is in a state of complete relaxation, are often as fruitful as those of physical activity.

'Fortune favours the prepared mind.'

Idea 84: Write down ideas

*I have never met a man so ignorant that I couldn't learn
from him.*

Galileo Galilei, Italian astronomer

Richard Branson, founder of the Virgin group of companies, always
keeps a notebook in his pocket in order to write down ideas. It is a
wise habit for any leader or manager.

If you are a good listener you will soon net plenty of fish – fish of
all shapes, sizes and varieties. Besides providing you with the
stimulus to think for yourself, other people can also give you plenty
of new ideas to work on. We certainly need this kind of outside
stimulus that only comes from other minds. Lord Thomson of Fleet
showed the way:

> *The way I look at it, everyone has an idea and one in a dozen
> may be a good idea. If you have to talk to a dozen people to
> get one good idea, even just the glimmering of an idea, that
> isn't wasteful work.*
>
> *People are continually passing things on to me, because I
> have given them to believe that I will be interested, I might even
> pay for it! Sometimes, usually when it is least expected, some-
> thing comes up that is touched with gold.*

Never complain about a lack of ideas! If you don't have them, go out
and talk to those who do – even though they may lack your power
to make them happen. St Augustine of Hippo once said: 'I learn most,
not from those who taught me but from those who talked with me.'

Use your notebook of ideas as a tool for creative reflection and thinking. Creativeness is bringing together things that conventional

thought considers unrelated into new relationships. 'A person who can create ideas worthy of note,' said Konosuke Matsushita, 'is a person who has learned much from others.'

If your mind is questioning and curious – taking everything interesting as grist to its mill – diverse images, concepts and ideas can come together in fertile and stimulating ways. Give it a try.

Idea 85: How to improve your creativity

Mankind is pre-eminently creative, destined to strive con-sciously for a purpose and to engage in making – that is, incessantly and eternally to make new roads, wherever they may lead.

Fyodor Dostoevsky, Russian writer

One of the most valuable principles for improving your creative approach to work and life is to learn to *think outside the box*. Essentially that means being willing to challenge the assumptions, often unconscious, that put an invisible cage around the bird of thought.

Making analogies is often the trigger for new ideas. Creative thinking often begins with the perception of a relation – a spark of meaning – between two apparently unrelated things or ideas.

Really creative people have a *wide span of relevance*: they look far afield, even to remote places or times in history, for solutions to the problems.

There is a danger in formalizing any aspect of the creative process. It is a delicate balance between following a conscious process or framework and being guided by the mind's natural inclinations. But it is worth bearing in mind the common-sense sequence that we saw in Idea 80:

◆ Preparation
◆ Incubation
◆ Insight
◆ Validation

Never forget the creativity that lies within other people, like the sparks from a flint. Strike the flint and you will have fire.

New ideas are essential to all human enterprise. *Creativity is about having new and valuable ideas; innovation is about bringing them to market in the form of improved or new products and services.*

The universal need for innovation in industry and commerce, coupled with the fact that quite small changes can save costs or improve products, opens the door of creativity to all who care to enter.

The same principles apply in innovation as in creative thinking. Improvements may lie far afield in another country, another technology or even another time in history.

Innovation is an act that strives to produce small improvements on what is accepted today. It sees newer and better solutions to old and current problems, solutions tied to a practical objective and geared to a measurable operational result. The development of the digital clock is a good example.

Most change is incremental rather than discontinuous. Innovation means not merely introducing novelties but making changes to something that is already established. An example of this more modest kind of creative change was the adding of milk to chocolate by Daniel Peter in 1867 to make milk chocolate.

> **Remind yourself**
> The need for innovation is universal. All products, whether goods or services, require continual renovation and improvement. Change is happening all around us and it can suddenly outflank whole technologies.

> *'Standing still isn't an option.'*

Idea 86: Suspend judgement

Criticism often takes from the tree caterpillars and blossoms together.

Jean-Paul Sartre, French philosopher

The best-known and most widely used creative thinking technique is brainstorming. It was introduced in the 1930s, so it has been around a long time – a sign of its usefulness. You can employ its principles when you are thinking alone, but they work better in a small group.

The essential principle behind brainstorming is simple, namely that you should concentrate on the spontaneous flow of ideas and suspend judgement on them until later in the process. By analogy, turn the hot water tap on full and turn off the cold tap. If you run them both together you get tepid or lukewarm water. What the first rule of brainstorming commands you to do is in fact, if you think about it, to make a temporary and conscious division between the mental function of *synthesizing* on the one hand and *analyzing* and *valuing* on the other. In the wrong hands, valuing is so often both negative and premature. Like unseasonable frost it kills off the creative buds of new ideas.

You can, of course, apply this principle in your own thinking and in conversation with friends, as opposed to more formal or structured brainstorming sessions. Bear in mind what Einstein said once to a friend: 'If at first the idea is not absurd, then there is no hope for it.'

Exercise: Brainstorming skills
Take a pair of scissors and list 50 new uses for them, apart from cutting things. You have 10 minutes. Write your ideas down. If you get stuck, here is a practical tip: go back and build on your first 10 ideas. The world record is 596 ideas.

Idea 87: How to lead a brainstorming session

The best way to get a good idea is to get lots of ideas.

Linus Pauling, US chemist and peace activist

No more than 10 people should be involved in a brainstorming session. Some may know about the field you are thinking about, others may not; a mixture of both is desirable. They should ideally have been trained in the brainstorming technique before the meeting. When you run the sessions:

◆ Define the problem (using your analytical and briefing skills).
◆ Help people to understand the problem by highlighting the background information and history.
◆ Clarify the aim in a succinct sentence: 'In how many ways can we . . . ?'
◆ Have a brief warm-up session, using a common problem or object.
◆ Brainstorm 70 ideas in 20 minutes, or a similar target. One person should write up the ideas on a flipchart. Allow time for silent reflection. Check that no critical remarks are made. Encourage cross-fertilization.
◆ Establish criteria for selecting feasible ideas. Choose the best.
◆ Reverse brainstorm: 'In how many ways can this idea fail?'

About 40 minutes is the optimum time for a brainstorming session. However, you should ask the participants to go on considering the problem after they leave and let you have further suggestions.

Remember that they have programmed their depth minds by the brainstorming session, and other ideas will come to them unexpectedly.

Case study: Jigsaw puzzles

A leading US firm of jigsaw puzzle makers held a brainstorming session to think up ideas for new puzzles. It produced some worthy ideas but nothing brilliant. A month later, one of the participants went to see an exhibition of Tutankhamun's treasures in Washington, DC. The gold mask of the pharaoh struck him as a great jigsaw puzzle idea! He was right – it broke all records for jigsaw puzzle sales in the United States.

Guidelines for brainstorming

Suspend judgement	Give imagination the green light by withholding the critical evaluation of ideas until later. Accept ideas without judging them.
Welcome freewheeling	Take off the brakes in your mind and go with the flow of your ideas. The more unusual the idea, the better – it is easier to tone down than to think up.
Strive for quantity	The greater number of oysters, the more likely you are to find some pearls in them.
Combine and improve	Listen to the ideas of others and see if you can build on them. Their way-out ideas may stimulate some buried memories or sleeping brain cells in your depth mind.
Do not edit	Ideas should not be elaborated or defended, just quickly stated and recorded.

One major reason why brainstorming is useful is that it helps to free us from a 'functional fixedness'. We have a fixed idea, for example, that a thing has only one function and that is what it is there for. By banning that familiar function (in the case of scissors, the function of cutting), the mind is released to consider other possibilities. With a little adaptation, scissors would make an interesting geometrical instrument.

Take the modern British Army bayonet. Did you know that it is ingeniously designed to combine with its scabbard to form a pair of wire cutters? Or that it has a third function (officially!) built into it – that of a bottle opener!

Case studies

Pilkington Brothers in the UK had a technical problem. During the final inspection of their sheet glass, small globules of water were identified by the inspection machine as flaws in the glass. A brainstorming session produced 29 ideas for solving this problem in less than five minutes. After some research and development, three of these ideas were used in the system, which solved the problem.

H. J. Heinz in the USA had a marketing problem. The company wanted to get sales promotional material to consumers more quickly. Brainstorming produced 195 ideas. After evaluation, eight were immediately used. A member of Heinz, when talking about another brainstorming session, said: 'Brainstorming generated more and better ideas than our special committee produced in 10 meetings.'

Idea 88: Ten questions for entrepreneurs

We must obey the greatest law of change. It is the most powerful law of nature.

Edmund Burke, Irish statesman and author

Creative thinking is fun, and it can also lead to the development of some interesting new products and services. Wearing the hat of an entrepreneur, should you invest your own money in any given proposal?

1. Is it really new?
2. Is it both relevant and practical?
3. Whom will it involve?
4. How much will it cost?
5. How much will it save?
6. Will it require more testing or evaluation?
7. What is the best profit margin?
8. Can it be easily copied by competitors?
9. Does it have a patent?
10. Are the management team behind it of high calibre?

All proposed innovations within organizations or institutions need to be subjected to the same rigorous evaluation. As a manager you are responsible for investing stakeholders' money wisely, not wasting it on new products and services that are doomed to fail.

Idea 89: How to encourage innovation

Not geniuses, but average men require profound stimulation, incentive towards creative effort, and the nurture of great hopes.

John Collier, US social reformer

What can you do as a manager to encourage innovation around you? Here are some practical steps:

◆ Set an example by thinking about your own job and making some improvements. Remember, activity is not the same as action. Ships are not the only things that collect barnacles. Scrape them off your keel. If you change yourself, you will trigger change around you.

◆ Look at your work team with a new eye. Sort out the innovators from those who have lost their entrepreneurial drive. Encourage each individual to come up with a quota of ideas.

◆ Work out a fair system for rewarding both the creative individual and the creative group. An incentive scheme can help, but make sure that you keep it alive and well.

◆ Set aside time now and then for meetings designed to think creatively about innovations. Bring to these meetings a list of suggestions or problems submitted by individuals for discussion. Take action on suggestions that seem promising.

◆ Develop an atmosphere of trust and warmth, a supportive and constructive climate where individuals are encouraged to think for themselves.

◆ Ideas rarely arrive in this world fully formed and gift-wrapped. With a little practice you can learn to *build on ideas*, to take the germs of success in someone else's half-baked idea and develop it towards fruition. By the same warrant, allow others to build on your ideas for the common good.

◆ Creativity is so delicate a flower that praise tends to make it bloom, while discouragement often nips it in the bud. *Any of us will put out more and better ideas if our efforts are appreciated.*

Follow-up test

Productive thinking

☐ Do you have a reputation for 'thinking outside the box'?
☐ Have you made a practice of always testing assumptions in order to eliminate the false ones?
☐ Are you fully aware of the effect that negative criticism can have on half-formed ideas?
☐ Would you describe yourself as a holistic thinker?
☐ Do you make full use of your imagination?

Useful originality

☐ Is your depth mind creative in the way it fuses together things that are apparently completely separate?
☐ Can you recognize instances when the creative thinking process has worked for you?
☐ Are you able to brainstorm ideas when you need to do so, both on your own and with others?
☐ Have you created a climate or atmosphere in your organization that positively encourages and supports innovation on all levels?
☐ Is your team noted for its creative ideas and willingness to try new ways or methods?

☐ Are you aware that you may have a set of unconscious assumptions that could be barriers to creative thinking?

☐ Do you sometimes consciously use your imagination when considering options in any given decision-making situation?

☐ 'The most original person is the one who borrows from the most sources.' Can you develop new ideas on a wide range of sources?

PART FIVE

Practical Wisdom

'Thought.' D.H. Lawrence wrote, 'is a man in his wholeness wholly attending.' In other words, it is a holistic concept. It is the whole person who thinks and decides, faces problems and comes to terms with reality.

And as wholes we *grow* like trees throughout our lifetime. Our body, of course, changes and shows its age. Our leaves go brown at the edges and our branches splinter. But our mind can go on from strength to strength, and in some cases it bears that most valuable human fruit of all – practical wisdom.

Not that practical wisdom is the prerogative of age. As the proverb reminds us: *There is no fool like an old fool*. But experience of life is a key ingredient in practical wisdom, and that tends to come only over time. It was not, after all, the young Winston Churchill who wrote: 'Perfect solutions to our difficulties are not to be looked for in an imperfect world.'

Reflective thinking is the key. It helps you to turn the products of many flowers, some sweet and some bitter, into the honey of practical wisdom. But you have to do that work, for no one else can do it for you. As the Italian poet Petrarch said:

> Take care that honey does not remain in you in the same state as when you gathered it: bees would have no credit unless they transformed it into something different and better.

Eleven Greatest Ideas for Practical Wisdom

Idea 90: Time to think

If you want to be successful as a leader – an equation that entails being successful as a decision maker – you have to create for yourself time to think. Given the pressures of top jobs, where the urgent constantly drowns out the important, that is no easy task.

One of the most impressive leaders I have known personally was Field Marshal Lord Montgomery. He taught me that any leader in a high position must be ruthless about one thing: the use of their time. Listen to him for yourself.

Case study: Making time to think

What advice can be offered to a leader? He must discipline himself and lead a carefully regulated and ordered life. He must allow a certain amount of time for quiet thought and reflection; the best times are in the early morning, and in the evening.

The quality, good or bad, of any action which is to be taken will vary directly with the time spent in thinking; against this, he must not be rigid; his decisions and plans must be adaptable to changing situations. A certain ruthlessness is essential, particularly with inefficiency and also with those who would waste his time. People will accept this, provided the leader is ruthless with himself . . .

Most leaders will find there is so much to do and so little time to do it; that was my experience in the military sphere. My answer to that is not to worry; what is needed is a quiet contemplation of all aspects of the problem, followed by a decision – and it is fatal to worry afterwards.

Field Marshal Viscount Montgomery

Ask yourself
Do I set aside a time each day 'for quiet thought and reflection'?

Idea 91: Reflective thinking

All the troubles of life come upon us because we refuse to sit quietly for a while each day in our rooms.

Blaise Pascal, French philosopher and mathematician

I use the term 'reflective' thinking to cover the mental activity required to ask searching (and sometimes embarrassing) questions about the adequacy of the current operation.

This kind of thinking can be disturbing to some managers at the centre of successful action, because they may see it as dealing with remote abstractions, with theories of management that seem impractical, and with visionary speculations about the future.

The success of a business today, largely based on action thinking, gives the opportunity to build vitality but it doesn't do the building. For that reflective thinking is essential.

It is always possible to reach your immediate goals without a great deal of reflective thinking. But you need reflective thinking to build vitality for tomorrow, for this is the way you will get a deeper understanding of your problems.

I make this point because I believe that the pressures to meet the problems of the day tend to discourage reflective thinking, and when this happens to any business it will surely lose vitality. Doesn't this apply to your business, too?

Reflective thinking can also restore *your* vitality as a leader. It's no good trying to shine if you don't take time to fill your lamps.

Idea 92: Ten principles of time management

You can ask me for anything you like, except time.

Napoleon Bonaparte, French military
leader and Emperor

Here is a practical framework to remind you of what you as a leader and manager should be doing strategically to make the best use of your time. I am assuming that you have long since mastered the tactics of doing so.

1. *Develop a personal sense of time.*

   You cannot afford to waste your own time or allow others to waste it, wittingly or unwittingly. That doesn't mean, however, that you become a kind of time miser, grudging every minute. The object is to be able to spend time freely, generously and spontaneously. You have heard of 'value for money' – get 'value for time'.

2. *Identify long-term goals.*

   You need to identify the *ends* of your strategic thinking and to be able to express them to yourself in simple terms. Do you have a vision, four or five open-ended aims and a set of defining values? These will serve as guidelines for how you should be spending your time.

3. *Make middle-term plans.*

   Organizationally, this is the realm of strategic planning: establishing the goals and objectives – specific, time-bounded, realistic, stretching and exciting – that are the concrete destination, like towns and cities, that the chief parts of the organization need to get to on the road that your long-term thinking has identified.

4. *Plan the day.*

It is essential for you to have a clear plan in mind for each day, preferably made the day before. At the level of strategic leadership you need an excellent personal assistant (and supporting staff in a large organization). With such a PA it is comparatively easy to work out a system for managing your diary, and this makes planning each day for maximum effect a lot easier.

5. *Make the best use of your time.*

Reserve high-quality time for thinking time. By that I don't mean necessarily being on your own. Thinking time in strategic leadership involves others, either a small group or individuals. What matters, however, is that subjects that demand creativity, wisdom or imagination are not left as an afterthought at the end of a gruelling ten-hour day, or just before you leave for the airport.

6. *Organize office work.*

You need appropriate staff to handle your administrative affairs, and a room where you can work quietly on your own and hold meetings with small groups (preferably with a round table) or individuals (comfortable chairs round a coffee table). However, the less time you spend in your office the better. When asked why he was so rarely behind his desk, the president of Toyota replied, 'We do not make cars in my office.'

7. *Manage meetings.*

Meetings should begin on time and end on time. Your skills as a leader of meetings need to be well honed, for you will find yourself chairing plenty of them. If you can be brisk and businesslike yet gracious and courteous, the business gets done and people will look forward to your meetings.

8. *Delegate effectively.*

   The golden rule of time management for strategic leaders! The main candidates for delegation are the more managerial parts of the role. Yet delegation should never generate into abdication, the vice of mentally slothful senior managers. You should have a passion for good administration and really value those who deliver it.

9. *Make use of committed time.*

   Julius Caesar dictated to five secretaries who accompanied him on horseback as he rode on his campaigns; his equivalent of a mobile phone. Waiting time – for example when someone is unavoidably late for a meeting in your room – gives you some minutes to check a letter or read a paper. During a busy day, committed time does yield these pockets, five minutes here, ten minutes there, which can all be put to use. *Look after the minutes and the hours will look after themselves.*

10. *Manage your health.*

    Being a strategic leader in today's changing world is a demanding role: you need to be mentally and physically fit. Energy, vitality and resilience can only be sustained by adequate sleep, temperance and taking sensible exercise.

Idea 93: Intellectual humility

It ain't what you don't know that gets you into trouble. It's what you know for sure that just ain't so.

Mark Twain, author of *Huckleberry Finn*

The world's two greatest teachers on leadership – the near contemporaries Socrates in Greece and Confucius in China – were agreed on one thing: the need to distinguish clearly between what you know and what you don't know. And, of course, that it is essential to avoid the arrogance of claiming to know something that you do not in fact know. In other words, stick to the truth.

To accept that one may have been wrong after a decision and to accept the consequences form one aspect of adhering to the truth.

To be open to others and their ideas before a decision means that you do not believe you are a genius who alone knows what to do; this is an equally important facet of humility. It is as the Scottish proverb says: *The clan is greater than the chief.* A chief who believes this is more likely to consult the clan and listen to their ideas. The author G.K. Chesterton once said, 'It is always the secure who are humble.'

The principal intellectual contribution of humility to the mind of a leader is that it signifies a marked lack of self in mental perception and calculations. Self is like an overpresent shadow; it can obscure the clarity of the mind.

Putting it another way, if you and I could but see reality as it is – not just that which presents itself to our senses – we should reflect it as humility. Conversely, the more humble we are, the more likely it is that we shall see life and its changing situations and other people *as they really are*. Humble people are standing in front of their own shadows. They clearly see relations and proportions within the scheme of things.

That is why intellectual humility is such an important ingredient in practical wisdom. Fortunately it is accessible to us all, not least because life conspires to make us humble in the end. 'The only wisdom we can acquire,' said T.S. Eliot, 'the wisdom of humility.'

'We are all worms, but leaders are called to be glow-worms.'

Idea 94: Foresight

> *A man may prophesy,*
> *With a near aim, of the main chance of things*
> *As yet not come to life, which in their seeds*
> *And weak beginnings lie intreasured.*
>
> William Shakespeare, *Henry IV*

Foresight means to know or expect that something will happen or come into existence in advance of its occurrence. That sense of 'things to come' is derived from your ability to draw inferences or make projections from the present but at a depth mind level – intuition.

Ask yourself
In my field of business, what is coming next after what is coming next?

According to the historian Thucydides, none surpassed the Athenian statesman and general Themistocles in practical wisdom, which included foresight:

> *Themistocles was a man who showed an unmistakable natural genius; in this respect he was quite exceptional, and beyond all others deserves our admiration.*
>
> *Without studying a subject in advance or deliberating over it later, but using simply the intelligence that was his by nature, he had the power to reach the right conclusion in matters that have to be settled on the spur of the moment and do not admit of long discussions, and in estimating what was likely to happen,*

his forecasts of the future were always more reliable than those of others.

He could perfectly well explain any subject with which he was familiar, and even outside his own department he was still capable of giving an excellent opinion.

He was particularly remarkable at looking into the future and seeing there the hidden possibilities for good or evil.

To sum him up in a few words, it may be said that through force of genius and by rapidity of action this man was supreme at doing precisely the right thing at precisely the right moment.

That ability to do 'precisely the right thing at precisely the right moment' – and, one might add, in precisely the right way – is a very good working definition of what practical wisdom means.

The short-range weather forecasts, however, are much more reliable than long-range ones.

Therefore, in Winston Churchill's words:

It is a mistake to think too far ahead. Only one link in the chain of destiny can be handled at a time.

Idea 95: Calm judgement

> *Reason and calm judgement, the qualities especially belonging to a leader.*
>
> Tacitus, senator and historian of the Roman Empire

As a leader, you need to remain calm at all times. By calmness here I mean not exhibiting visible tension or excitement when such reactions might well be expected in the circumstances. As Rudyard Kipling put it:

> *If you can keep your head when all about you*
> *Are losing theirs and blaming it on you.*
> *If you can trust yourself when all men doubt you,*
> *But make allowance for their doubting too;*

Cool, calm and collected: these words are often bracketed together as a phrase. They suggest that a leader's mental resources are completely intact in the face of difficulty. *Calm* stresses a quiet approach to a problem, devoid of hysterical actions or utterances, while *collected* emphasizes the application of practical reason to the solution of the problem.

To be free from agitation of any sort in the face of danger or provocation, to be able to concentrate the mind, eliminating distractions, especially in moments of crisis: these are indeed qualities essential in any leader of stature.

As the seventeenth-century French writer Voltaire said of John Churchill, first Duke of Marlborough, he possessed 'that calm courage in the midst of tumult, that serenity of soul in danger, which the English call a cool head'.

Case study: Coolness in action

General Robert E. Lee was perhaps the finest military leader in the American Civil War. At the outset both sides sought him as their Commander-in-Chief, but Lee's loyalty to his native state of Virginia drew him into the camp of the Confederacy. By skilful generalship and good leadership he waged a remarkably successful war against the North. But at the three-day battle of Gettysburg any hope of victory for the South virtually disappeared. The decisive point in the battle came when an attack led by one of Lee's subordinates, General Pickett, failed. An eyewitness was present when news of this disaster reached Lee:

> *His face did not show the slightest disappointment, care or annoyance, and he addressed every soldier he met with a few words of encouragement – 'All will come right in the end, we'll talk it over afterwards.' And to a Brigade Commander speaking angrily of the heavy losses of his men: 'Never mind, General, all this has been my fault. It is I who have lost this fight, and you must help me out of it the best way you can.'*

Idea 96: Learning from experience

I have learned throughout my life as a composer chiefly through my mistakes and pursuits of false assumptions, not by my exposure to founts of wisdom and knowledge.

Igor Stravinsky, Russian composer

Can you learn to have better judgement? The answer is plainly yes, because we do in fact get better at decision making. You will learn comparatively little from the decisions you get right; a great deal, however, from the decisions you got wrong.

The key to learning is to identify – in your own reflective thinking or with the help of others – the *lessons* that this unpleasant experience has to teach you. It is by this method that you build up your own body of knowledge about how to think clearly, to make decisions and solve problems, to involve others in the right way, to generate your own ideas and to listen to the ideas of others.

All that a book like this one can do is to cut down the time that you take to learn from experience. It does so by offering you *principles* to consider. Learning happens when the sparks jump between principles and experience, theory and practice.

We cannot be taught wisdom, we have to discover it for ourselves by a journey which no one can undertake for us, an effort which no one can spare us.

Marcel Proust, French novelist

Idea 97: People decisions

Intuition is a clear conception of the whole at once.

Johann Lavater, Swiss theologian

'Selection of top management is probably the most important of all decisions – for example, about board membership. A is retiring, in four years' time: B and C follow soon after. Who are the likely candidates? There is now time to position them so that the experience will equip them for the board.'

So said the chairman of a company to me the other day. People decisions of this nature – not to mention other, more personal ones, such as whether or not to marry a particular person – are immensely important, both professionally and personally.

The implication of this model is that we 'get to know' people as 'wholes'. This contrasts with the dominant analytical approaches today. Yet thinking of others as collections of assessable traits, such as you find in the various packaged forms of 'psychometrics', doesn't really work.

There is plenty of room for more exploration by observation of the ways in which people do get to know each other. But it is already clear that a good judge of people considers the whole and not the parts.

The role of the depth mind

We take in far more information about other people, especially as we get to know them better, than our conscious minds can handle. So our depth mind processes and digests it for us, and occasionally provisional conclusions float to the surface of our mind in the form of intuitions.

Exercise

Draw the lines of this diagram, one at a time in the order they are numbered. As you draw each one, look at what you have drawn and write briefly what is there.

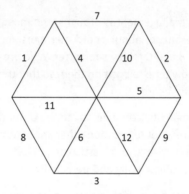

Most people find that at certain stages they see a well-known shape developing, and succeeding lines confirm and support this.

But there are stages when they are taken aback by the next addition, and find that the earlier pattern has to be replaced by a new one.

This demonstration will, of course, undoubtedly lose by being presented in this way, where the end state can be seen. Even so, it may be worth going through the steps yourself, even though you know the result, in order to see what I mean. Or why not try it on someone who does not know the final appearance?

The novels of Jane Austen are justly famous because they describe how a young woman's judgement of a man can alter and develop as she gets to know him better. Both reason and intuition are at work. And eventually the heroine finds that, to her delight, her mind has made itself up. He is the right person for her.

> *'When reason and intuition agree, you know that you are on the right road.'*

US management consultant and academic Peter Drucker wrote in *The Effective Executive* (1967):

> *Among the effective executives I have had occasion to observe, there have been people who make decisions fast, and people who make them rather slowly. But, without exception, they made personnel decisions slowly and they make them several times before they really commit themselves.*

Idea 98: Judgement

Learning is not wisdom; information does not guarantee good judgement.

John Dewey, US educational reformer

Judgement is the quality of mind or character that enables you to make the right choices or decisions, or to reach intelligent conclusions.

It is not to be confused with either *knowledge* or *experience*. You can have one or both of these in buckets and still lack judgement.

Judgement seldom applies to an inborn quality, though it usually suggests a foundation of native good sense. But it also suggests intellectual qualities, such as the discernment of facts or conditions that are not obvious, as well as knowledge of those that are ascertainable.

Together with these skills goes an ability to comprehend the significance of those facts and conditions and to draw correct, unbiased conclusions from them. Training, discipline and experience are the key actors in the shaping of your judgement.

Idea 99: Three elements of practical wisdom

A great alchemist created the gold of practical wisdom by fusing in the crucible of his imagination *intelligence*, *experience* and *goodness*.

The Greeks had a word for this combination of intelligence, experience and goodness in practical affairs: *phronesis*. This was translated into Latin as *prudential* and thence into English as *prudence*. A better translation today is *practical wisdom*.

Intelligence

In this context, to be intelligent means to be able:

- ◆ To see the point.
- ◆ To sense relationships and analogies quickly.
- ◆ To identify the essentials in a complex picture.
- ◆ To 'put two and two together'.
- ◆ To find the salient factors in past experience that are helpful in shedding light on present difficulties.
- ◆ To be able to distinguish clearly between ends and means.
- ◆ To appraise situations swiftly.
- ◆ To see their significance in the total setting of present and past experience.
- ◆ To get the cue as to the likely line of wise action.

These overlap considerably, but taken together they offer an idea of the kind of intelligence or *sense* we are talking about.

Experience

In the list above the interdependence of *intelligence* with *experience* is evident. Experience can be either experience of life in general, which of course comes only with age, or relevant experience to a given situation.

Familiarity here is based on considerable actual practice. You have personally encountered, undergone or lived through situations not unlike the one now faced. By implication, this past immersion in a subject or field has resulted in superior understanding.

Sometimes, however, gain in wisdom need not be suggested by the word so much as a piling up of involvement. Marshal Saxe's donkey, it is said, went on twenty campaigns carrying his master's baggage, but learned nothing about the art of war!

Goodness

The Greeks sensibly had two different words for good: *kalos* (skilled in, proficient at) and *agathos*.

In Homeric times, to enquire if a king leader was *agathos* meant was he courageous, wise and kindly? In other words, did he fight, manage and rule with success? Virtue or normal excellence referred to his art or skill in performing his socially allotted role.

Later, *agathos* came to refer not to the qualities required to fulfil a role but to certain human qualities that we call *goodness*.

The element of *goodness* in wisdom could almost be described as *character*. By saying that a person has *character* (as opposed to *personality* and *temperament*) we mean that they have:

◆ A conception of what they should be and what others may rightly expect of them.

◆ Principles that they will not likely betray.
◆ Loyalties and commitments of an enduring kind.
◆ Firmness when subjected to attractive temptations.
◆ Responsibility for their own actions and an expectation
  that others will be responsible too.
◆ A sense of the reality of moral values, so that they are
  not a matter of personal preference.

Idea 100: Your path to practical wisdom

Practical wisdom is only to be learned in the school of experience. Precepts and instruction are useful so far as they go, but, without the discipline of real life, they remain of the nature of theory only.

Samuel Smiles, author of *Self-Help*

If you wish to be effective as a practical thinker – a contributor to the world's business – you need to set aside time for reflective thinking. You need to give yourself time to think.

Be as clear as possible about what you do know and what you don't know. Opinion is not the same as knowledge. Intellectual humility is your greatest insurance policy against making a fool of yourself.

It is wise to think ahead in order to foresee change. It is always better for your organization to take change by the hand before it takes you by the throat!

Manage or control your emotions, so that you remain calm. This optimizes your chances of making the right decisions. Your example will calm others down, too, so that they can think and act coolly under pressure.

People decisions are best taken slowly. Use your powers of observation and reason; listen to your intuition. If reason and intuition agree, go ahead.

Experience tempers and improves your judgement, but you need intelligence and goodness as well for *phronesis*, practical wisdom.

Follow-up test

Practical wisdom

☐ Do you create sufficient times for quiet and calm, reflective thinking on what you are doing and what you could be doing?

☐ Are you a master of time management?

☐ Are you aware when people are making claims to knowledge that they don't have – even when you are the speaker?

☐ What is your record in judging people? In selecting and promoting individuals, which of the following statements characterizes your approach?

> ☐ You can always pick a winner, and never consult anyone else or seek specialist advice.
>
> ☐ You go by first impressions. Even if you think you are wrong you usually return to them in the end.
>
> ☐ You take people-decisions slowly. You like to consult others who know the person, often on a confidential basis.
>
> ☐ You do not trust your own first thought.
>
> ☐ You like to see a person in a variety of different situations before making up your mind. Track record is an important factor to you, more so than psychological tests and the like.
>
> ☐ You rarely choose a person on technical grounds alone, unless they are working on their own. You try to see them in the context of being a team leader or member, and

judge whether they will get on well with the individuals in that group.

☐ How do you rate yourself as far as judgement in decision making is concerned:

◆ Good: Your decisions usually have the predicted results, you can foresee consequences and are rarely surprised at outcomes. You are shrewd and discerning at all times.

◆ Average: Your predictions of consequences are accurate about half the time. Your common sense is often proved right.

◆ Weak: Poor judgement often mars your performance. You tend to guess too much what will result from a given decision, and are frequently wrong.

☐ Can you think of two individuals you know – a man and a woman – who show in their lives and business practical wisdom, that rare combination of intelligence, experience and goodness?

Appendix:
Solutions

Idea 1: Who owns the zebra?

This problem can be solved by analytical and logical thinking – deductive logic – and persistence! It is necessary to compile a matrix.

Roughly halfway through the problem-solving process there are two forks in the road, or mental leaps. The only way to find out which way to go is by trial and error. If you choose the wrong road, you have to retrace your steps. You can see now why the world record for finding the solution is 10 minutes!

The following is one way of solving the problem.

Keep working through the facts from 1 to 15 in sequence.

Concentrate on clues for which there is only one answer. That is:

    1   There are five houses, each with a front door of a different colour, and inhabited by people of different nationalities, with different pets and drinks. Each person eats a different kind of food.

    9   Milk is drunk in the middle house.

   10 The Norwegian lives in the first house on the left.

   15 The Norwegian lives next to the house with the blue door.

Then look for information that has only two possible answers. This is the first mental leap. That is:

    6   The house with the green door is immediately to the right (your right) of the house with the ivory door.

If you place the ivory door in the middle, with the green door on its right, the answer is wrong, but you can still progress to find out who drinks the water. However, you can go no further.

If you place the ivory door in the fourth house, with the green door on the far right, this answer is correct and you can progress logically, since you will find that other items of information now have only one answer. That is:

2 The Australian lives in the house with the red door.
4 Coffee is drunk in the house with the green door.
8 Apples are eaten in the house with the yellow door.
12 Apples are eaten in the house next to the house where the horse is kept.

Then look for information that has only two possible answers. This is the second mental leap. That is:

3 The Italian owns the dog.

If you place the Italian in the house with the green door you are wrong, but you can still find out who drinks the water.

If you place the Italian in the house with the ivory door you are correct and you can progress logically, since you find that other items of information now have only one answer. That is:

5 The Ukrainian drinks tea.
13 The cake-eater drinks orange juice.

Therefore the Norwegian drinks water.

14 The Japanese eats bananas.
7 The mushroom-eater owns snails.
11 The person who eats onions lives in the house next to the person with the fox.

Therefore the Japanese owns the zebra.

Another way of solving this problem is to form a matrix using nationalities rather than house numbers:

Front doors	yellow	blue	red	ivory	green
Inhabitants	*Norwegian*	Ukrainian	Australian	Italian	*Japanese*
Pets	fox	horse	snails	dog	*zebra*
Drinks	*water*	tea	milk	orange juice	coffee
Food	apples	onions	mushrooms	cake	bananas

Idea 67: The nine dots and the six matches

Brainstorming challenges one kind of unconscious assumption, namely that hammers are for knocking in nails or that scissors are for cutting. But there are other forms of unconscious assumption that may inhibit your thinking.

Take the 'Nine dots' and 'Six matchsticks' problems in Idea 67. The reason so many people cannot do the first one is that they put an unconscious or invisible framework around the dots, and try to solve the problem within it. That is impossible. But if you break out of that self-imposed limitation, the solution to the problem is easily reached.

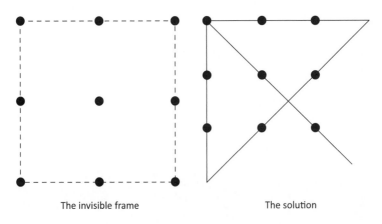

The invisible frame   The solution

The nine dots solution

Incidentally, I first published the nine dots problem in 1969, in a book called *Training for Decisions*. It was the origin of a new phrase in the English language, now credited to me: *thinking outside the box*.

There is a similar assumption made in the six matches problem. People *assume* that they must arrange the six matches in a pattern of four equilateral triangles in only one plane. If they take one small step and give themselves permission to place the matches on top of one another, they can reach the first solution. But if they break out of the two-dimensional constraint into three dimensions, they achieve the most elegant solution.

Form the matches into a pyramid. The problem cannot be solved on one plane alone; you have to break out into three dimensions. Used immediately after the nine dots it is interesting to note whether or not students can see any relation between them.

Idea 82: Inventions and developments

1 A young English designer named Carwardine approached the firm of Herbert Terry at the beginning of the 1930s with the proposal that it should build a desk light employing the constant-tension jointing principles found in the human arm. The company agreed, and the Anglepoise light was the result. From that time it has been in production, scarcely altered except for details and finishes.

2 Cat's eyes in the road.

3 Spitfires.

4 Clarence Birdseye took a vacation in Canada and saw some salmon that had been naturally frozen in ice and then thawed. When they were cooked he noticed how fresh they tasted. He borrowed the idea and the mighty frozen food industry was born.

5 They could have suggested the principle of independent suspension.

6 The burrowing movement of earthworms has suggested a new method of mining, which is now in commercial production.

7 In the Royal Botanic Garden in Edinburgh there is a plaque commemorating a flower that inspired the design of the Crystal Palace.

8 Sir Basil Spence, the architect of Coventry Cathedral, was flipping through the pages of a natural history magazine when he came across an enlargement of the eye of a fly, and that gave him the general lines for the vault.

9 Linear motors.

10 Ball-and-socket joints.

About John Adair

John Adair is the business guru who invented Action Centred Leadership (ACL) in the 1970s, now one of the best-known leadership models in the world. Organizations worldwide use it to develop their leadership capability and management skills. ACL is being successfully applied in engineering companies, retailers, local authorities, financial institutions and universities. The British armed services base their leadership training on it.

John's company, Adair International, provides ACL development programmes, Accredited Trainer programmes and consultancy around the world, via regional partnerships with training providers in the UK, Australia, New Zealand, the Middle East and India.

John is the author of more than 40 books, translated into many languages, and numerous articles on history, leadership and management development.

Index